HE'S RIGHT HERE

BY

MARGARET C. MCGEE

Dear Dr Conway,
    Thank you for your interest
in my book. Seems like "yesterday"
when you and I had a little conversation
on "write a page a day and it will get done."
    It's been an amazing accomplishment
for me and I want to say again.
Thanks for all your encouraging
words! God bless you always,
        Love, Maggie McGee
                9-12-12

Copyright © 2011 by Margaret C. McGee

First edition

Scripture passages were taken from:

The Way, The Catholic Living Bible copyright 1974, 1989 by Tyndale House Publishers, Inc., Wheaton, Illinois. Printed in the United States of America.

The Life Recovery Bible, New Living Translation, copyright 1998, Tyndale House Publishers, Inc., Wheaton, Illinois. Printed in the United States of America.

Published by Margaret C. McGee

ISBN

978-1-257-92213-0

Printed in the United States of America

By lulu.com

Brendan Michael McGee
November 26, 1975 – September 11, 2003

Table of Contents

DEDICATION

First and foremost, I give thanks to The Holy Spirit, Who has inspired me with a passionate desire to write this book.

After September 11th of 2003, I spent many hours in front of the Blessed Sacrament at a small chapel close to my home. It was a place of consolation and solace, where I found peace and quiet and where my wounded heart was healed…very gently…very gradually, one day at a time. It was a place I could empty myself before the Lord and tell Him exactly how I was feeling, and never once did I ever question His Mighty Presence! Therefore, it is with gratitude in my heart that I write this book, all to the honor and glory of God!

I would also like to dedicate this book to my children and grandchildren. There are no words to describe the overflowing love I have for them and how grateful I am each day of my life.

Of special importance and to whom I also dedicate this book, is my wonderful mom. Throughout her life, she has taught me so much, by her genuine love and strong faith.

Last but not least, I dedicate this book to my husband, Bob who has always patiently and lovingly stood by me with his encouragement and honest advice. He is indeed my greatest support and my pillar of strength. Often, I call him "the wind beneath my wings."

ACKNOWLEDGEMENT

On New Years' Eve, 2009, I made a quick phone call to my longtime friend, Fr. Lyons. After wishing him a Happy New Year, I told him about my exciting plans to write a book. I explained that I wanted to help other parents who have also suffered the loss of a son or daughter to know that eternal life is real and we will see our loved ones again. I know this to be true, especially because of the many profound experiences I have had since the tragic, unexpected loss of my youngest son, Brendan. Then Fr. Lyons commented how eternal life can be represented by a Christmas wreath; "The birth of Jesus is the beginning and there is no end."

Then, on January 7, 2010, I began to talk with my co-worker Tracy Darcy about my plan to write a book. I had made a list of possible titles and I said to her, "All I know is he's right here." She repeated it back to me …"That's it! He's right here!" From that day on, I knew it was a perfect title to engage many readers.

I will always remember a conversation I had with Dr. John Conway. He was very supportive as he said to me, "Write one page a day and it will get done." Thank you for such great advice and encouragement! Since this was to be my first book, I truly appreciated this wise suggestion, and it filled me with renewed enthusiasm.

On May 30th, 2010, I sat and talked in length to my friend, Carol Taormina, about my passion to write this book. I expressed my desire to speak to the hearts of those who are hurting, through my own personal experiences. I also alluded to specific verses in the Bible that directly apply to these experiences.

Carol looked me in the eyes and said with all sincerity, "I see it already happening; I can see you doing your book signing!" What a vote of confidence she gave me! Her words were spoken with affirmation and assurance, which gave me the continued hope I needed to venture upon this journey of new beginnings, which I began to see as a reality.

These stories may seem absurd to some but will be

consoling and comforting, and will give renewed hope to those having a similar heartbreaking experience and perhaps feeling there is no way out.

I would like to thank my friend, Maureen Lamoureux, for all those times she sat and listened with love and compassion. It was always a pleasure to sit and talk with her whenever our paths crossed. I specifically remember an occasion when we met for lunch and I shared a few of my very moving experiences with her as she listened intently. "You tell your stories with such passion," she commented. "I know you will definitely help other parents who read your book." Her positive affirmations certainly were appreciated and I am very grateful.

My dad was well-known for saying, "Write it down, it's a good one!" Every now and again, as I'm deep in thought trying to find the words to describe a particular story in my book, I hear his voice just an arm's length away, supporting me, rooting for me and encouraging me to "write it down, it's a good one!" Although no longer with us, it's important for me to say, "Thanks Dad!"

Thanks and praise also goes to my mom, who willingly and faithfully proofread each one of my stories as they were compiled. My mom has always enjoyed reading and now at the age of ninety, it remains one of her favorite pastimes. I thoroughly cherished her ideas, suggestions and encouraging words as we sat together many an afternoon reviewing what I had written. It was a wonderful experience and one I will always treasure!

I will be forever grateful to Dr. Joseph Coyle, a Christian psychologist, who I was privileged to meet at a conference when he spoke on the topic of "dealing with loss and grief." I was immediately impressed with his spiritual approach. His gentle demeanor, compassion and strong faith encouraged me to surrender my pain and sorrow to a loving God, using his suggested imagery technique. With newfound hope and enthusiasm, my idea to write this book became a reality. The truth has set me free!

I owe a debt of gratitude and appreciation to my very thoughtful niece, Melissa McLaughlin, for her editing expertise. Melissa spent many long hours, carefully and professionally reviewing my manuscript and giving me many helpful suggestions to make my book a great success.

Last but not least, I would like to sincerely thank my friend, Robin, for all she has done for me. My first introduction to Robin was in the year 2001 at Saint Patrick's Church where I was attending a charismatic prayer meeting. In February of 2002, I attended a Life in the Spirit Seminar and chose Robin to be my prayer sponsor. Quite ironically, I was at this same prayer meeting at Saint Patrick's Church where Robin is a member of the prayer team, on the night of my son's car accident. (You will read about this night, in the chapter entitled, Little Did We Know).

After praying about a very important decision regarding my book, I was inspired to make a phone call to Robin. On that same day, she kindly offered me her services! Just a week later, as we sat together in front of my computer, while Robin was explaining the formatting of my book, I realized that computer technology was her field of expertise! Who knew! I will always remember her encouraging words: "God bless the work of your hands." I believe Robin's help and encouragement was all part of God's perfect plan. With her patience, love, generosity and God's sufficient grace, she helped me to follow my dream and publish my first book.

Chapter 1 - The Early Years

On the 26th day of November of the year 1975, Brendan Michael McGee was born. What amazes me is that I can still remember the details of that evening like it was only yesterday. At about five o'clock in the evening, I knew I was in labor and needed to get to the hospital. My dad volunteered to come over and take care of my four year old son, Robbie, and my two year old daughter, Lisa. I was so happy to see his smiling face. After greeting my husband and me at the front door, he gave us his blessing and off we went to the hospital. In the labor room, a Bruins game was airing on television, so in between my contractions, my husband was checking the score! Five hours later at 9:51 P.M., Brendan was born. As I held my newborn son in my arms and kissed his face, it was one of the happiest moments of my life! About seven minutes later, the Boston Bruins won the game! I can still recall the loud cheering during those moments of exquisite joy!

At one month of age, Brendan was diagnosed with pneumonia and was admitted to the hospital, just a few days before Christmas. Amongst the stuffed animals of years past, sits a little brown teddy bear that still plays "rock-a-bye-baby!"

A year later, on the 1st of December, our family moved to Boise, Idaho. We drove for four days with our three children in the back of our newly bought Oldsmobile station wagon! Brendan was a very happy, content baby and was easily entertained by his four year old sister and six year old brother.

About six months later, we drove across country to Parkersburg, West Virginia. Brendan loved being outdoors and he would spend hours at a time in his playpen, totally content, watching our neighbors skateboarding up and down the walkway.

In the summer of 1978, we drove back to our home in Massachusetts for a visit. Brendan was three years old. For as long as I can remember, he always loved little puppies, so he was in his glory when we were given a Samoyed Husky pup to bring back to our home in West Virginia. Brendan and Asia became great pals! Wherever Brendan was, there I would find Asia lying beside him.

In June of 1979, we packed our family into our "faithful" Oldsmobile station wagon and moved to Arizona. I must admit, it was quite a feat traveling with the newest member of our family, our year old, white, fluffy-haired Samoyed! In human terms, he was probably saying, "What a revolting development this is!" Thankfully, he was a good traveler and we made it to Arizona in three days.

When Brendan was four years old, he attended Mary Moppet's Nursery School in Glendale, Arizona. I was attending classes at Glendale Community College and Brendan thought it was absolutely wonderful that he was going to school as well, "just like Mom." It certainly didn't take much to please him! Recently, my mother reminded me of the summer we visited Disneyland, and Brendan smiled for days after he got to see the real Mickey Mouse! Today, whenever anyone speaks of Mickey Mouse, she smiles and thinks of Brendan.

On his fourth birthday, I brought a cake to his school and all his little nursery school buddies sang happy birthday to him! His face was beaming with excitement as if to say, *"All this for me?"* He made friends easily and already had lots of them! Indeed, it was his special day! Amongst my fondest memories is what Brendan was wearing that day; it was a light green plaid jacket with light green pants to match and a light green bow tie, neatly clipped to the collar of his shirt. How adorable he looked! Now and again, I reflect upon that day and all the cherished memories I hold so dear to my heart. Throughout his lifetime, birthdays remained a special celebration.

At the age of five, Brendan learned how to swim. He loved swimming in our pool and jumping off the diving board! I can still picture him swimming underwater and after every couple of feet, his head would pop up for air! I remember the summer he thought he had forgotten how to swim! I reassured him he would remember once he dove in….and he realized he didn't forget after all!

Brendan also enjoyed playing baseball every season. He especially enjoyed playing when his dad was the assistant coach. I have an old photograph of the two of them, which is one of our many treasures.

As Brendan grew older, his interests included Cub Scouts and Boy Scouts. While still in Cub Scouts, his brother Rob was a member of the Boy Scouts so Brendan was privileged to go on camping trips with them. Brendan was always very proud of his older brother. I remember the Pinewood Derby they attended each year when Brendan had the opportunity to build his own car for the derby race. What fun he had!

During his years in scouting, he won many trophies and earned several awards, including an "Ad Altar Dei" religious award. In English this means, "To the altar of God," which is a program for Catholic scouts who wish to increase their knowledge of the Faith. We were so proud of him when he chose to prepare for this award! Set upon a shelf in "Brendan's room" are many of his activity badges, his Arrow of Light Award, several of his trophies and the many cars he entered into the Pinewood Derby races. Recently, while looking through his merit badge books, I got a little teary-eyed as I remembered him proudly reciting the Scout Law. As I read the following words, I could almost hear his voice echoing back to me…

"A scout is trustworthy, loyal, helpful, friendly, courteous, kind, obedient, cheerful, thrifty, brave, clean, and reverent." I'm sure that anyone who knew Brendan would agree; he definitely was all of the above. Additionally, words taken from the Scout Oath, *"to help other people at all times,"* was something Brendan took very seriously and was always considerate of others' needs before his own. From very early on, I often heard people say, "There's something special about Brendan." Yes, indeed there was!

In 1986, we moved back to Massachusetts. Brendan became very interested in playing the drums and started taking drum lessons. We surprised him with his first set of drums on Christmas Day. I will never forget the expression of excitement and pure joy on his face! We have a collection of photographs of Brendan and his drums, neatly arranged in a picture frame on the wall in "Brendan's room," attesting to his passion for music. Playing the drums became one of his greatest pleasures for many years.

I'll always remember the day my daughter, Lisa, brought home an adorable, six week old German Shepard puppy we named Molly. Right away, Brendan fell in love with her and everywhere that Brendan went, Molly would follow. She soon learned who she could depend upon for all her needs. Brendan enjoyed her company as much as she enjoyed his! Molly especially loved going for walks, sometimes carrying her own leash in her mouth, as she trotted down the road with Brendan by her side. It was quite a sight to see! Who was leading who!? She also enjoyed playing ball with us as we ran around the yard together. Brendan's natural ability to care for both Asia and Molly, plus his dedication, love and compassion for animals led him to believe that perhaps one day he would become a veterinarian. I know he would have made an excellent one, but his idea never came to fruition.

Over the years, Brendan and Asia had also become very attached to one another. Sadly however, Asia had developed diabetes and eventually was nearly blind. As Molly grew older, it was as if she knew Asia needed her help, and she would stop and wait for him, as the two of them made their way up the stairs or out to the back yard. She appointed herself "Asia's personal guide dog," it seemed. Sometimes she would nudge him to play but Asia was losing interest and didn't have the spunk he once had. It was as if Molly understood and we would find the two of them nuzzled next to one another.

This brings me back to when Brendan was about ten years old and we were at a family gathering. We had recently moved back to Massachusetts after living in West Virginia and Arizona for the past several years. He talked to my older brother, John, and my sister-in-law, Brenda, for quite a long time and at the end of the conversation he said to my brother, "By the way, who are you guys anyway?!" My brother still reminisces about that day. We all miss him so very much!

In 1987, Brendan became an altar server at Saint Rose of Lima Church. He and our pastor, Father Lyons, developed a special relationship with one another. Beginning in the fifth grade and on through high school, Brendan was honored to assist Father Lyons each Friday evening during Lent, as he proudly carried the five foot tall crucifix during the Stations of the Cross. Whenever Brendan wanted to discuss an important issue, he knew he could always count on Father Lyons for advice and counsel. They became great friends.

On through the years, Brendan continued his service at Saint Rose of Lima Church and on October 18, 1992, he received the Sacrament of Confirmation. On that memorable occasion, his Uncle Tim was his Confirmation sponsor and he chose the name, Blaise, for his Confirmation name, after his Uncle Blaise. This was a great honor for both my brothers!

I specifically remember the precise moment Brendan was confirmed when the Bishop made the Sign of the Cross with chrism oil on his forehead, signifying Brendan was now "a soldier for Christ." Then the Bishop smiled and said something as he shook Brendan's hand. I wondered what he said, because I distinctly remember I didn't see the Bishop say anything to the other confirmation candidates who were in line just ahead of him. To this day, that little gesture remains in the forefront of my mind. I believe it had special meaning but perhaps I will never know.

Vicki and her family also attended Saint Rose of Lima Church. Vicki's mom, Janet, and I sang in the choir together and Janet would often speak to me about Vicki's interest in Brendan. "She used to stare at him when he was serving Mass," Janet said. "Being three and one half years younger than Brendan, she figured he would never notice her." It wasn't until much later that they actually met and developed a relationship with each other. A few years later, they were engaged to be married.

Chapter 2 - The Later Years

One of Brendan's greatest enjoyments was playing his drums while listening to his favorite music. With drumsticks in hand, he would get lost in a world of sheer ecstasy! At one time his drums were set up in our sunroom. Our next door neighbors will always testify to this! Whenever I see Kris, she tenderly comments about the days when his drums could be heard throughout the entire neighborhood! I see tears in her eyes every time we talk about it. Then she comments about "what a nice kid he always was."

Brendan joined the Marching Band when he was in the ninth grade and continued playing the drums throughout high school. I can still clearly picture him at all the school concerts or marching with his drums across the football field at the start of all the games. Each year in our home town of Rochester, I recall the times he marched in the Memorial Day Parade starting at the town hall, past the cemetery where we now visit him and all the way to the baseball field. Then there were the Saint Patrick's Day Parades in Boston that he loved. Whenever I hear the sound of drums, I think of Brendan and I smile. Today, whenever our grandchildren start beating on Brendan's drums, I think to myself, "I'll bet

Brendan is smiling down upon them from heaven and giving them his blessing! Yes, he's right here!

Brendan had many friends, but his very best friend, without a doubt, was Donald. They remained best friends all through junior high and high school. They both enjoyed attending Phish concerts in Maine, fishing off Planting Island in Marion and sometimes partying until all hours of the night! And yes, you guessed it; wherever Brendan was found beating on his drums, there you would also find his buddy, Donald, joining him. It was a true and lasting friendship. Donald was devastated and heartbroken when he heard of Brendan's car accident. Placed in front of Brendan's memorial stone is a "Phish" key ring, in memory of all the great times they had over the years together. Each year at our annual music scholarship fund in memory of Brendan, Donald brings and sets up the tent, as a memorial gift in honor of his best friend. Whenever I see Donald, I give him a big hug. I think of Brendan and his awesome hugs and I remember how special Brendan was to him. When Donald stops by I feel Brendan's presence all around. Thank you Donald for your thoughtful and caring ways and for everything you did for Brendan. Donald knows he is welcome here anytime, as it is always such a pleasure to see him and his adorable son, Willie!

June 4, 1994 was Brendan's graduation day. It was a glorious, sunny afternoon. I was always so proud of his many accomplishments. I recall my own graduation ceremony from Glendale Community College, when Brendan's voice rang out through the crowd as I heard him say, "Go Mom!" He lovingly acknowledged my persistence and hard work that made my graduation a reality, while at the same time, fulfilling my role as "Mom." Spending time with my children was always very important to me.

After graduation, Brendan attended American International College in Springfield, Massachusetts. Still undecided of a definite career choice, he began by taking a liberal arts course. I remember saying, "Don't worry; you have your whole life ahead of you." He never really knew for certain what the Lord was calling him to be, although he had a lot of ideas. College life was not easy for him, as he was trying to find his comfort zone. Brendan had a generous and kind heart, a compassion for others, a desire to be instrumental and effective in everything he did. He set very high standards for himself and often had difficulty accepting that he couldn't **do** and **be everything to everyone.**

"I shouldn't take myself so seriously," he would say. We were so much alike! "Be gentle with yourself," I would tell him, trying to pass on to him, what I had just begun to learn.

After a couple years, he continued his studies at Bridgewater Community College.

Brendan truly loved landscaping. From the time he was about twelve years old, he enjoyed working outdoors and helping his dad, neatly edging and mowing the lawn, pulling weeds and caring for the flower beds. He took great pride in his work and our yard always looked beautiful when he was finished. Eventually, he worked fulltime for a landscaping company and thoroughly enjoyed it.

Another fun thing Brendan enjoyed doing was working out with his weights. I always knew when Brendan was at home because his music would be blasting! One of his favorite songs was Eye of the Tiger by the American rock band, Survivor. He also enjoyed listening to Creedence Clearwater Revival, Phish, Frank Sinatra, Aerosmith, Sarah McLachlan, Pearl Jam, Pink Floyd, and the Dave Matthews Band. The list goes on and on!

One of Brendan's favorite pastimes was rollerblading and it wasn't uncommon to see his nephews, Vincent and Brendan, riding their bicycles alongside of him. "Let's race!" they would say. Then while getting plenty of exercise myself, I would follow them down the road! It was certainly great fun. Time passes but memories stay fresh.

As silly as this may sound, one of the things I really appreciated about Brendan was his willingness to wash my car. He knew it was definitely not one of my favorite things to do and would often volunteer his services. He'd turn on the car radio and find something he liked to listen to and he was all set! I still think of him every time I drive into a car wash, something I never had to do when Brendan was around. How I miss him!

Another special person in Brendan's life, was Vicki, his

fiancée. What I remember most about their relationship was his thoughtful and caring ways to always bring her happiness. As their relationship grew, Brendan bought her a dozen, long-stemmed, red roses to commemorate each month they were together. It seemed we were always making room for these gorgeous flowers, in our refrigerator! "I have to keep them fresh until tonight," he would say.

As time went on, Brendan began an apprenticeship program for The International Brotherhood of Electrical Workers and studied to become a telecommunications technician. His graduation ceremony was on June 5, 2003, just three months before his tragic accident. On the 11th of September, Brendan was no longer with us.

Chapter 3 - Little Did We Know

On September 11, 2003, our lives were changed forever. Earlier that day, my son, Brendan and my husband, Bob, spent the day together working on the electrical wiring of our new home. Brendan decided to try out his new tools he had bought for his new job. The treasured memories of this day will live forever in my husband's heart.

Later that same afternoon, Brendan decided to take a drive and he stopped at the house where our family had lived for seventeen years, beginning when Brendan was a young boy at the age of nine. Upon entering, Brendan asked if he could explore his old home and the new owner gladly obliged.

"We had a long conversation, reminiscing about his many happy memories while he lived here." The new owner smiled as he spoke. He then told us how glad he was to meet Brendan, whom he met for the first time on this day.

At about 4:30 P.M. Brendan returned with an eagerness to get out the hoses and wash his Blazer! He took great pride and excellent care of his vehicle and really enjoyed keeping it clean, shiny and like new; it was like a hobby for him! He drove up the driveway, walked up to me with open arms and gave me a big hug with a big smile on his face. However, this hug was "different." I didn't know its significance at the time, but the memory of it is implanted deeply in my heart. It is something I have reflected upon for the weeks, months, and years that have followed. I can still hear his voice like it was yesterday and I often sense his presence close by. As he gathered the hoses to wash his Blazer, we discussed his exciting plans to start a new job the next morning. I was very happy for him and I said with great enthusiasm, "Praise God," and raising his arm into the air, he shouted "Yeah!" Everything was finally falling into place for him and he was overjoyed. At about 5:30 P.M., I ventured out for my usual walk. As I waved good-by, I glanced at him in the garage putting everything away, including a newly bought long-handled brush he used for that one day. Today, it is another precious keepsake and a memory I hold dear to my heart.

Later that evening, Brendan went to visit his sister, Lisa and his two nephews, Vincent and Nicholas. He later went out with Lisa to buy a special birthday gift for Vincent and found a pair of Batman pajamas, just what Vincent requested! On the way home, he made a peculiar comment to Lisa by saying, "I'm so cold" even though it was unusually warm that evening. She said his voice sounded like a little kid's voice. When it was time to leave her house that evening, he seemed hesitant, like he had something he had left to do. She reminded him that his older brother, Rob, was expecting him soon, as it was getting late and he was bringing his nephew, "little Brendan" home with him. (He was living with his brother while our new house was being constructed). He gave his sister, and nephews, Vincent and Nicholas, a big hug good-by and left for his brother, Rob's home.

Meanwhile, I was attending a prayer meeting in Wareham as I often did on Thursday evenings. At about 9:30 P.M. the prayer team asked me if I wanted them to pray with me and I gladly accepted. I made a request they pray for my son, Brendan, who was to start a new job the next morning. Prayers were then offered for his success and I clearly remember hearing the words "abundant blessings," as they prayed over me.

At about 10:30 P.M., I returned to my daughter and son-in-law's home where my husband and I were staying during the construction of our new home. When I got there, my daughter, Lisa was pacing back and forth. "Something is wrong," she said. "I know it! Rob's been calling looking for Brendan. I told him they left at least an hour ago. I shouldn't have let him go! He was standing in the doorway and acted like he didn't want to leave." Again she said, "I shouldn't have let him go!" She was really upset.

I became very anxious and began to pray silently, "Please, dear Lord… let everything be alright," but I couldn't calm myself down.

About fifteen minutes later, we received a phone call from Brendan's fiancée. I could tell by the sound of her voice that something was very wrong. Her voice was shaky. "There's been a terrible accident! They've taken Brendan to the hospital. The policeman said little Brendan is okay. I'm on my way to the hospital….I'll meet you there, okay?"

I could barely breathe, let alone answer her. I began to shake and all I could say was "Oh my God, Vicki! Of course we'll be there! I just have to tell Bob…Oh my God…We'll meet you there!" I ran up to the bedroom to tell my husband who had just fallen asleep. "There's been a terrible accident!" I screamed. They've taken Brendan to the hospital and that's all I know. I began to cry hysterically. My husband was obviously very upset but tried his best to help me calm down.

(Just recently, he was able to tell me, "I didn't want to go; As soon as you came running into the room, I got a horrible feeling in my gut. I knew it was bad.")

"Come on!" I yelled. "We have to go **now!** We have to get to the hospital now!!" I frantically ran towards the front door.

With a look of panic on her face, my daughter, Lisa, exclaimed, "I'll call the emergency room and they'll tell me he's okay! They'll know he's my brother and they won't want me to worry. (Lisa was employed by Saint Luke's Hospital, and actually worked in the emergency room). Deep down inside she knew they wouldn't call …She knew everything was **not alright**. Lisa was originally scheduled to work this particular night, but about a week earlier, her schedule had been changed.

Seconds later, my husband and I were on our way to Saint Luke's hospital where we would meet with Vicki. As soon as we got there, I said to my husband, "Stop the car! I have to get out!" I couldn't wait another second!

Chapter 4 - Hearts Broken

As I charged into the entrance of the emergency room, I saw Vicki's mom, Janet. I heard the words "He's gone." I wanted to know where they took him! Again, I heard those piercing words which rang through my head. "He's gone!" It was too much to bear! My legs collapsed from underneath me. I began to scream at the top of my lungs, "No…No…No!" I couldn't take it! I was on my knees begging! Someone in a white uniform tried to hold me back. I yelled at him… "Where is he?! I need to see my son!" I tried to shove past him. Then a voice said, "it's okay, you can let her in."

I remember rushing into the emergency room totally overwhelmed at what was happening. Then I caught sight of my precious grandson, Brendan, sitting on a stretcher, his hands folded on his lap, with only a minor scratch on his forehead. I walked up to him as if in a daze. He looked at me with incredible love and compassion trying to comfort me, as he said,

"You don't have to tell me, Gramma; I already know; I saw Uncle Brendan's face." Then he paused as if to prepare me and said ever so gently, "and it was dead…really, Gramma……and I saw his hand… and it was broken." It was like he was trying to spare me the shocking truth and wanted to be the first one to break the terrible news to me.

Still, with his little hands folded on his lap, he said, as he looked into my eyes with inexpressible love and reassurance:

"But it's okay, Gramma…I saw the angels take him to heaven; I have him right here in my heart," as he placed both hands over his little chest.

I was stunned by these priceless words of wisdom coming from the mouth of my four and one half year old grandson, Brendan. I knew his Guardian Angel had to have been by his side, keeping him safe and protected at all times.

His dad, who was nearby, consumed with grief, was trying to console me, and said with deep sorrow, "I'm so sorry…I'm so sorry!" I vaguely remember saying to him, "My God, Rob, what are we going to do?!"

Then I turned around and walked towards my son, Brendan, a few feet away, lying on a stretcher. I remember seeing several nurses standing around him. I could see tears in their eyes. I knew they were devastated they couldn't save my precious son, also Lisa's brother. I looked at him lying there so still. The first thing I saw was an endotracheal tube in his mouth. I wanted to know all the facts. I noticed the "dying heart" pattern on the cardiac monitor rhythm strip. I asked the nurses if it was his but I already knew; they didn't have to answer me.

His skin was warm, his right arm was by his side and his left arm was crossed over his chest. A gauze was covering his left hand. I wanted to cup his head into my hands but I was told not to touch the back of his head because it was "injured." I didn't want to *hurt* him even more, so I decided not to lift his head. I touched his warm face, his lips and stroked his hair. Oh how I wish I saved a piece of his hair! It was a nightmare! I felt completely helpless!

"When you wake up I'm going to take you home," I said. (This I later learned from Vicki's mom, standing across from me).

Then I tried to hug him and said repeatedly,

"I love you, I love you, I love you... Oh my God...I love you so much!!!!!!!" The words just kept rolling off my tongue uncontrollably. I thought he appeared to be sleeping and he was going to wake up so I could take him home. If Brendan could speak, he would have said, "I love you too Mom. I'm not gone. I am with you always, so talk to me. I am listening."

Later I learned it was during the time I arrived at the emergency room and wanted to see Brendan, that Father Michael Racine had been with him while the nurses and doctors were performing CPR....Sometime later that night, Father Mike sat and spoke with me and I will always remember his profoundly consoling words....

"We prayed together," he said. "He knew I was there."

This moment in time will be with me forever. It was very important for me to know the actual time that Brendan was anointed and I specifically remember Father Mike told me, " It was about 10:45 P.M." Brendan was pronounced at 11:20 P.M. I remember thanking him repeatedly for this gift he had given to my son. I alluded to a "golden key," which I believed opened the gates of heaven unto him and I knew, beyond a shadow of a doubt, Brendan was safe in the arms of Jesus, his new employer, praying for all of us here on earth.

As I was leaving the hospital with my husband, son and grandson, I wanted so desperately to run back to Brendan's side to see and touch him one more time. It was like I was watching a very sad movie, unable to grasp or realize it was *my son,* I was leaving behind. It was excruciatingly painful to leave him. "I have to go back!" I said to my husband. It was so awful! I couldn't bring him home with me! The nurses had told me they would take good care of him and I trusted them and knew that they would. Somehow, I was given the strength to leave him, and very slowly, I walked out the door. Undoubtedly, the Lord had to have been carrying me that night.

We later gathered at my daughter and son-in-law's home, as we tried to console one another to make some sense out of what happened. We stayed up for the rest of the night just talking about Brendan...... Rob and Lisa's "little brother" was no longer with us. How could that possibly be?!

Chapter 5 - Saying Goodbye

Soon it was morning and the stark reality of Brendan's death surrounded me. The memory of the night before filled me with deep anxiety. It felt like a giant knot of intense pain was twisting around my heart and yanking it out. I felt an intense longing for my son. I wanted to go to him. I couldn't stand it. Then I wailed, "I can't do this!! Why did this have to happen!! What am I going to do!? Oh Lord, please help me! This is awful!" I began to cry and couldn't stop. Then, suddenly, I thought to myself, where **is** everybody? I had no idea what time it was. I crawled up from the mattress I had slept on and went downstairs. I was terribly concerned about my parents.

"We have to tell them in person!" I exclaimed to my husband. "We have to get to Saint Peter's Church so we can tell Mom and Dad about Brendan's accident; I don't want them to find out from someone else!" That was my main focus. We got ready and left for church.

"Let's come in from the back door," I suggested. "Then we can see where they are sitting and sit with them." In we walked and saw they were sitting in their usual seats up front. I was so emotional at that point and decided to sit in the back row. I didn't want to see or talk to anyone except my parents. As the Mass was being said, we realized my parents already knew, when the priest mentioned Brendan's name. My parents had received a phone call early that same morning from my sister, Melanie. Apparently, it was all over the newscast, which traveled rapidly throughout my family. Everyone was in the state of shock and disbelief. After Mass, my husband and I walked up to my parents. As their eyes met ours, there were no words to express our pain. They were devastated and their deep sadness was written all over their faces. I was very grateful to my parents and the kind and thoughtful priest who offered the Mass for Brendan. It was obvious to me he understood our pain and heartache, as he told us about his own experience of losing his only brother to a car accident. My heart was filled with compassion for him. Brendan was gone....gone from our lives. Nothing could change this horrible and cruel fact.

After Mass, we hugged both our parents and then drove home. The dreaded task of making the funeral arrangements was upon us. Just the idea of it sent shivers down my spine. We needed to bring Brendan's clothes to the funeral home. I remember finding his light grey suit hanging in his closet. It was neatly packed away in its zippered garment bag and Brendan had written, "Brendan's Gray Suite," on the outside of the bag. I still have that garment bag hanging in my closet and I know I will treasure it forever. I also thought it was very important to bring his favorite aftershave lotion because I wanted him to smell nice.

As soon as we arrived at the funeral home, I rushed right in and I remember asking, "When can I see him?" I wanted desperately to hold him! I ached for him! The kind funeral director explained to me that his body was brought to a medical examiner in Boston since it was an unexpected death.

"When will he be back?" I asked tearfully. "I miss him so much!" He was so incredibly kind, compassionate and understanding. I could see he felt my pain. My husband and I were numb with grief and being there to choose a *casket* for our beloved son was unspeakable! Aside from seeing his lifeless body lying on that stretcher in the emergency room, it was the most painful experience of my life! I truly don't know how my husband and I got through it without collapsing. Undoubtedly, God must have been very close by our sides.

As I write this piece of my book, I hear Brendan saying to me, *"I'm right here. I am with you all the time. Just close your eyes and feel my presence. I love you."*

Next, we went to the florist shop to order all the flowers. The owner of the shop was so sad to hear about Brendan's accident. She knew him well, since this was where he went quite often to buy flowers for Vicki while they were dating.

A few hours later, we returned to my daughter's home where we were staying. My grandson, Brendan was there as well as some of my sisters. Brendan then expressed to my younger sister, Angela,

"Aunt Angie, Uncle Brendan's in heaven, you know. I saw the angels take him to heaven." My sister answered him saying:

"That's good." Then with even greater persistence, he repeated what he had just said, not being satisfied with her response. He needed to reiterate to his aunt what he knew he had seen! She, too, was amazed at what this four and one-half year old child had experienced and then had shared with her.

I believe young children are very close to God and the angels, and they see so much more of the "unknown" because of their innocence, belief and childlike trust.

To this day, we don't know the identity of the woman who rescued Brendan through the shattered rear window of the Blazer, rolled over on its roof. The state police officer told us she was an off-duty nurse. Brendan told me, "An angel got me out."

Over the next couple days, my daughter and I went through my many albums of photographs to be displayed on a large poster board at the funeral home. I honestly don't know how we did it. Again, I'm sure it was the grace of God.

Today, I still have that same display of photographs on the wall in "Brendan's room." Very often, I find my grandchildren looking at the photos of their Uncle Brendan and we share little stories about what they remember about him. Every time I think about taking it down and putting the pictures away, I decide….not yet. Maybe I'll keep them up forever!

The day for the wake arrived. My heart was longing to see Brendan. I missed him so terribly. My emotions were running wild. I remember sitting upstairs in my grandson Vincent's room and I couldn't stop crying. Brendan and Vincent were on their way up the stairs and they caught me off guard. "What's the matter with Gramma?" Brendan asked. I heard Vincent answer, "She's really sad because of what happened to Uncle Brendan." As they entered the room, I wiped my eyes and gave them both a hug and told them how much I loved them and that it's good to cry when you miss someone. They both hugged me back and said, "I love you too, Gramma." I am so blessed to have them in my life. As they left the room, I began to feel better.

At 1:30 that afternoon, I arrived with my husband to the funeral home. I wanted to be there early so I would have extra time to spend with my son before the crowds of visitors would arrive for the 3:00 P.M. visiting hours. I felt an intense desperation imbedded within my heart to be with my son. I missed him so much and I couldn't stand being away from him. My husband dropped me off to return a little later with the rest of the family as we had planned.

As I walked toward the entrance of the funeral home, I met the very caring and compassionate funeral director standing outside. He smiled at me and said with such a kindness in his voice, "Someone has sent you a rainbow," as he turned to look into the sky. It had been raining earlier in the day, but by then, the sun was shining. Even today, when I see a beautiful rainbow in the sky, I believe Brendan is speaking to me and I always feel a warm blanket of love surrounding me.

I hesitated before I walked inside. My only focus was to see Brendan. I anxiously glanced across the room and I saw him lying there in the casket. I felt like everything was in slow motion. I felt numb while looking at my son lying so still. It didn't make sense to me! I thought to myself, "He still looks like he is sleeping. His face looks perfect without a scratch on it. How can this be real?" I felt a terrible anxiety come over me as I walked a little closer. "I miss you so much Brendan!" I forgot he wouldn't look the same as he did the last time I saw him. I touched his skin. It was cold and I realized my precious Brendan was really gone! Still, I couldn't accept this horrible truth. I felt numb as I stood by him. "I love you so much, Brendan! What am I going to do without you!?" I can't begin to describe how awful I felt!

Next I saw Brendan's fiancée, Vicki, huddled together with her mom, and Father Lyons was also there trying to console her. I wanted to let her spend as much time as she needed. After a few minutes, we stood together, next to Brendan. Vicki carefully placed her class ring on Brendan's finger and kept his ring for herself. It was terribly sad; it was all such a nightmare for all of us!

The next thing I remember was seeing my younger sister, Melanie, come into the room. I used to take care of her when she was a baby, and she in turn babysat for my three children. We both broke down in tears. She loved Brendan so much; it was almost more than she could bear.

I looked at my watch and saw it was 2:45 P.M. and I saw

long lines of people flooding the hallways. My son, Rob, was greeting everyone as they stood in line. During the evening, Rob listened to one story after another about Brendan. Everyone was in shock over the loss of his little brother. Rob kept saying, "He's in a better place," trying to cope as best he could.

Droves of people came to pay their respects. My friend, Pam, placed a rosary ring in my hands. "Hold onto this," she said. It was like she knew how special the Blessed Mother is to me and how much I needed her to wrap me in her mantle of love, especially today, which is also the feast of Our Lady of Sorrows. Even on that day at the wake, I identified with her terrible pain and sorrow she must have experienced at the death of her Son, Jesus, on Calvary. Sometimes the only way I can cope and feel comforted is by turning my thoughts to Mary and her sorrow.

I watched peoples' stunned faces and I felt their pain as they knelt before Brendan. Hundreds of friends, acquaintances and family members came up to me, expressing their deep condolences. I felt so loved. The lines continued until 10:00 that evening. I heard there were some visitors who never made it through the doors. That made me sad and I wished I had known this. I didn't want anyone being sent away. Although my feet were numb from standing for so long, I wanted to be there to greet any number of people who came. I sincerely appreciated every embrace, every mention of Brendan and every kind word spoken. In my guest book I have written, there were sixteen hundred and twenty visitors who passed through that evening in addition to other people who sent flowers, cards, or messages.

Exhausted and emotionally bankrupt, we arrived home from the wake and were gathered together at my daughter and son-in-law's home. My son-in-law had just offered us something to eat. One thing I will remember forever is what happened next. Suddenly and unexpectedly, at exactly 11:25 P.M., the fan of their microwave oven came on with an unusually loud sound. We all jumped as we were completely startled by the loudness of the fan. Immediately I thought to myself, "Brendan is saying hi to everyone because that is something he would do!" Completely caught off guard and stunned by it all, Leigh said to us, "That fan hasn't worked for months!" Then he tried to turn it off. I said to

Leigh, "Don't try to turn it off. It will go off when Brendan gets his message across."

Then, another spontaneous thought ran through my head—that it was Brendan, joyously acclaiming to all of us how surprised and happy he was by the hundreds of friends and family who came to offer their condolences and say their last goodbyes to him. He was completely amazed as he was made aware that so many people loved him so very much! On this night, Brendan realized how many lives he touched, how special everyone perceived him to be, and the difference his life had made. I can still very clearly visualize myself standing in awe and brimming over with emotion, in front of the microwave oven because I knew deep within the confines of my heart, Brendan was right there speaking to me!! I believe that is also what truly kept me from falling apart that night. Then, just as abruptly, at 11:28 P.M., the fan went off.... by itself....and there was total silence because we knew Brendan **was** with us and everyone was speechless. It was like "a moment of silence" for him. There are no words to describe this powerful and profound moment, except that it is one I will remember forever.

A few minutes later, as my daughter went out to her back yard, the outside light came on. Astonished, she looked up. She knew Brendan was lighting her way. That light had not worked properly for at least two weeks or more. As I stood on her porch, I looked at her and agreed it was her brother protecting her. Once again, we both knew he was right there. I knew then as I know now, Brendan's spirit was present to all of us that night as it remains with us always and he wants us to know and believe this with faith and conviction. We were all totally mesmerized by the evening's events and the ways Brendan was letting us know he was all around us trying to comfort us, although in ways our human minds will never understand. We sat and talked for hours into the night and eventually said goodnight to one another realizing we needed to get some rest. While thinking of Brendan and unable to grasp what the next day would bring, I fell asleep.

Brendan's funeral Mass was at 11:00 the next morning. As our family gathered in the front pew directly in front of the Blessed Mother, my husband looked at her and said to me,

"She's got him," as he referred to her outstretched arms.

Our friend Jack gifted us with his beautiful voice as he sang the comforting words to the songs we carefully selected, most especially, the words to "Ave Maria," which deeply touched the hearts of everyone present.

The final hymn was "The Irish Blessing," as holy water was sprinkled over Brendan's casket. That's when I completely lost all control and when I couldn't pretend any longer. After Mass, with my arm draped across my son's casket being wheeled down the aisle, I sang those very meaningful words, "Till we meet again," to my son. Although tears were flowing down my face, it was extremely important that I sing all the words of the song **to him**, words that profoundly spoke what I felt at that moment. Somewhere in the depths of my heart, I heard him say, "I'm right here, Mom. I love you. I am with you now and I will be with you forever."

At the cemetery, I remember watching crowds of people listening to our friend, Father Kopp, who was trying to console everyone, as he spoke about the promise of eternal life.

I remember walking around feeling oblivious as to what was happening. I was on the outside looking in. Nothing was registering anymore so I just stood there and waited for it to be over.

Chapter 6 - The Fascination of a Fly

On September 16, 2003, our family gathered at my brother Tim's house after the funeral Mass of my beloved son, Brendan. As I sat by myself in the solarium, I noticed there was a fly buzzing round and round, caught in the fluorescent light bulb in the far corner of the room. It probably sounds strange and a bit weird, but for some reason, I couldn't keep my eyes off this frustrated fly.

I never thought another thing about it until a day or two later, when I was at Saint Rose of Lima Church, attending a nine o'clock Mass. I found incredible comfort being in this church. I sat and admired the beautiful, colorful, fresh-smelling flowers, remaining from Brendan's funeral Mass, still in front of the altar and the statue of the Blessed Mother.

During Mass, as I sat in the pew, a little fly landed beside me and then flew by me. Again, I didn't think much about it until the priest said to the congregation:

"I don't want you to think I'm having a seizure or anything, but there is this annoying fly that keeps hitting me in the face!"

Later, when I was about to receive the Eucharist, there it was again, flying in front of my face! After Mass, I went into the restroom and a little fly was chasing itself in the mirror!

Before I left the church that morning, I had a chance to have a little chat with the priest. He usually stopped to talk to me and inquire how I was doing since the loss of my son. I appreciated that so very much. He truly empathized with me, as he shared some of his own personal losses and grief experiences. As silly as this sounds, I was compelled to talk to him about this bothersome little fly. After our little discussion, as he was about to leave, he turned to me and said with a silly grin on his face, "So… do you think your son came back as a fly?!" Then, of course, we had a good laugh about it and I felt much better!

Some people talk about seeing a butterfly, a dragonfly or a hummingbird, which for a particular reason reminds them of their loved one. Brendan knows that ordinarily I can't stand flies and I was always running around with a fly swatter or a newspaper! He always loved joking around and now the joke is on me!

Perhaps he was telling me these little flies are God's little creatures and to go easy on them! All in all, I believe he wants me to smile and know he is very, very happy with his new job in heaven while watching over us and assuring us we will all be reunited someday.

Several months later, my sister, Angela, gave me a copy of this poem, written by William Blake entitled,

"The Fly"

Little fly, thy summer's play,
My thoughtless hand has brushed away.
Am not I, a fly like thee?
Or art not thou, a man like me?
For I dance, and drink, and sing;
Till some blind hand, shall brush my wing.
If thought is life, and strength and breath,
And the want of thought is death;
Then am I, a happy fly, if I live, or if I die.

I found this very interesting and it gave me a whole new attitude and respect for all God's creatures, including insects!

In chapter 12, entitled "*You're Not Like Me Yet,*" you will be amazed as you read an analogy made by my six year old grandson, Vincent, as he tells his very personal and moving story.

Some of the events or stories written in this book can certainly be classified as unexplainable, peculiar or unimaginable. However, this being said, they *did* happen and they *are* real, for me as well as for others, and I have been truly blessed and privileged with God's graces, to put these puzzling, yet true stories in print. Hence, my hope is for the reader to identify with one or more of the following stories and be touched in a powerful and special way as I have been.

Chapter 7 - Inspirations of Healing

A couple months had gone by since I had lost my son, Brendan, to a car accident. My husband and I were living with my daughter, Lisa, her husband, Leigh and their two children, Vincent, age five years and Nicholas, age five months. It was late in the evening on November 19, 2003. I remember glancing at the clock in my room. It was 10:05 P.M., which was the same hour my son, Brendan's accident had occurred on September 11, 2003. For as long as I can remember, it has always been very important for me to record the date and time of certain events or occurrences that have special significance. As I was yearning and searching for answers that night, I began to look through the pages of the Bible, which had become a regular practice for me since my son's accident. My first introduction to the Bible had begun just a couple years earlier, at a time when I had a strong desire in my heart to read and understand the Scriptures. On this particular evening, I was reading from "The Way, An Illustrated Edition Of The Catholic Bible." I began to feel a sense of hopefulness because I knew in my heart I would be provided with what I needed, and as I was drawn to certain chapters and verses, I received the answers to the many questions nagging at my heart. I randomly opened my Bible to Ezekiel, chapter one and began to read. The words grabbed my attention and I just kept on reading while looking for "something," although I didn't know what that "something" was. I firmly believe the Lord knew what I needed as I read the following:

"One day late in June, when I was thirty years old, the heavens were suddenly opened to me and I saw visions from God. I saw in this vision, a great storm coming toward me from the north, driving before it a huge cloud glowing with fire, with a mass of fire inside that flashed continually, that shone like polished brass. Then, from the center of the cloud, four strange forms appeared that looked like men, except that each had four faces and two pairs of wings.

The four living beings were joined wing to wing, and they flew straight forward without turning. Each had the face of a man (in front), with a lion's face on the right side (of his head), and the face of an ox on the left side, and the face of an eagle at the back! Each had two pairs of wings spreading out from the middle of his back. One pair stretched out to attach to the wings of the living beings on each side, and the other pair covered his body. Wherever their spirit went, they went, going straight forward without turning" (Ezekiel 1:2-6, 9-12).

For reasons unknown to me at the time, I felt inspired to continue reading. My heart was crying out for answers, wanting to know that my son was not alone at the time of the accident, and hoping to learn more, I eagerly read the following:

"As I stared at all of this, I saw four wheels on the ground beneath them, one wheel belonging to each. The wheels looked as if they were made of polished amber, and each wheel was constructed with a second wheel crosswise inside. They could go in any of the four directions without having to face around. The four wheels had rims and spokes, and the rims were filled with eyes around their edges. When the four living beings flew forward, the wheels moved forward with them. When they flew upwards, the wheels went up too. When the living beings stopped, the wheels stopped. For the spirit of the four living beings was in the wheels; so wherever their spirit went, the wheels and the living beings went there too. The sky spreading out above them looked as though it were made of crystal; it was inexpressibly beautiful" (Ezekiel 1:15-22).

I felt my heart beating in my chest! I knew this was written for me. I could visualize myriads of angels in and around the wheels of my son's Blazer on the night of his accident and I was compelled to read more! Having no idea what I was about to read next, I came upon these powerful words:

"When the Guardian Angels stood still, so did the wheels, for the spirit of the Guardian Angels was in the wheels. Then the glory of the Lord moved from the door of the Temple and stood above the Guardian Angels. And as I watched, the Guardian Angels flew with their wheels beside them to the east gate of the Temple. And the glory of the God of Israel was above them." (Ezekiel 10:17-19).

I was totally in awe and brimming over with emotion, and

I ran downstairs to show what I had read to my daughter! My heart was infused with anticipatory joy and I could hardly speak! With a look of amazement on her face, all my daughter could say was, "Wow!" She agreed the wording was quite profound and the look on her face was confirmation for me. I was certainly convinced my son, Brendan, was completely surrounded and ministered to by his own Guardian Angel and the Archangel Michael. After reading these verses, I also knew "the glory of the Lord" was indeed with him! I knew this in my heart, soul, mind and body with every fiber of my being, as I felt my heart leap in my chest!

I felt eternally grateful my four year old grandson, Brendan, was totally protected by his own Guardian Angel and numerous other angels all around as he was rescued from the wreckage. At the time of the accident, he was riding in his car seat sitting behind his Uncle Brendan. I vividly recalled what he had said to me that night at the hospital: "Gramma, I saw the angels take him to heaven." This was a confirmation for me as I read from the book of Ezekiel these words for the very first time in my life. I was convinced the Guardian Angels played a major role and were present and powerful on that night of September 11, 2003. A couple days later, my grandson said to me: "Uncle Brendan held onto me until he knew I would be alright. My godfather saved me, Gramma."

Though unseen by the human eye, God was present in unimaginable power and glory!

My son's Chevrolet Blazer, which he was driving, was the color of dark blue sapphire. These words caught my eye, as I read with enthusiasm these two short verses:

"For high in the sky above them was what looked like a throne made of beautiful, blue sapphire stones, and upon it sat someone who appeared to be a Man. From his waist up, he seemed to be all glowing bronze, dazzling like fire; and from his waist down he seemed to be entirely flame, and there was a glowing halo like a **rainbow** all around him. That was the way the glory of the Lord appeared to me" (Ezekiel 1:26-27).

I believe through Divine Intervention, I was inspired to read all these Scripture passages and I knew my son was safe in

God's loving care. My heart was at peace, for I knew he was born into eternal life on September 11, 2003. Interestingly enough, sapphire is the birthstone for September!

Seven years later, on March 21, 2010, an amazing revelation occurred when my grandson, Brendan, and I were attending Mass at Saint Francis Xavier Church in Acushnet. Looking at the stone column just in front of our pew, Brendan said: "Gramma, This church has some interesting detail." On the uppermost part of the column were the carvings of the face of an ox, a lion's face, an eagle's face and the face of a man, describing what I had read from Ezekiel chapter 1, verses 9-12, on the evening of November 19, 2003. I was amazed! He was especially interested in the eagle and asked me what it meant. I told him I had remembered reading about it in the Bible, but would have to investigate since I couldn't recall where exactly I had read it. My grandson was satisfied with my answer, but it wasn't until today, on April 16, 2010, as I write this book, that I can clearly see how everything ties together; I remembered the verses from the prophet, Ezekiel, describing the "four faces of the four Guardian Angels." I suddenly felt enlightened and later explained to my grandson these "four faces" are linked to the four evangelists: Luke, with the face of a winged ox; Matthew, with the face of a winged man; Mark, the face of a winged lion; and John, the face of a winged eagle. It is amazing to me that my grandson, Brendan, noticed and pointed out the "interesting detail," as he so wisely described it that morning. Otherwise, I might not have ever put it together.

One morning after Mass, as I was praying in the adoration chapel of Saint Francis Xavier Church, I was in awe as my eyes caught sight of the beautiful stained-glass windows having upon them the faces of a winged man, a winged lion, a winged ox, and an eagle! Along the side of each window was the name of the respective evangelist, namely, Matthew, Mark, Luke and John. Once again, I believe the Lord was speaking to me as he wanted me to see in beautiful color, what I had read months ago in November of 2003.

Several days later, during the week of school vacation, I brought my grandsons, Vincent, Nicholas and Luke, to morning

Mass with me, as I often do. I felt very inspired to ask them if they would like to go into the chapel to see for themselves, what I had learned and then had explained to them. My grandson, Vincent, was very receptive to my suggestion, and as we entered the chapel, the warmth of the candles filled the room; I could strongly sense the Lord's loving invitation! Vincent asked if he could light a candle and he and his younger brother, Nicholas, lit the candle together and said a prayer for their Auntie Sharon who was very ill. Then Vincent knelt in front of the statue of the Blessed Mother and Nicholas knelt before the statue of the Sacred Heart of Jesus. It was not until this tender moment that I realized how very special this opportunity was for both of them as they knelt with their heads bowed in prayer. When I had offered to bring my grandsons to the chapel, I had no idea it would leave such a meaningful impression upon them. And even though Luke was only two years old, he still remembers that day, and sometimes asks if we can "light another candle." (Lighting "birthday candles" and blowing them out, is one of his favorite things to do!) I am so very grateful to the Lord for the opportunity I was given on that very special day, and for His guidance and direction every day of our lives. Without a doubt, it is Jesus who deserves all the honor and all the glory with everything I do, especially whenever I am with my grandchildren. "I can do all things *through Christ who strengthens me"* (Philippians 4:13).

I would like to close this chapter of my book with the following beautiful words, which really spoke to my heart with the earnest hope they will also soothe another mother's heart, as they did mine. The following words are taken from the May, 2006 issue, of "Living Faith."

"We are like a child in its mother's womb. The infant lives and moves and has its being in the mother, and the mother, through her life blood, is in the child."

These words really touched my heart and reminded me of being Brendan's mother, feeling privileged to give him his life here on earth. Although he is separated from the physical world, he will continue living through me in spirit. I believe he has entered into eternal life where Mary is his heavenly mother and where he and I will reunite, face to face.

Chapter 8 - A Special Birthday

I remember it was a Saturday night in September of 2003, just about a week after the funeral of my son, Brendan, and I was by myself in my daughter's home. I can't actually remember where the rest of the family happened to be, but I do remember I needed this private time for myself to somehow be in touch with what I was feeling. Time seemed to stand still as I watched the rest of the world pass by and I needed to stop and breathe!

I was missing Brendan so terribly and couldn't stop thinking about him. I missed his special hugs and his physical touch! In my solitude, I began to glance through the pages of a booklet containing Scripture verses, for those mourning the death of a loved one, given to me by my friend, Peggy. It was as if Brendan opened the booklet *for me,* to the very page I was about to read. It was written as follows, and I quote:

"I am the resurrection and the life; whoever believes in me, even though he dies, will live, and anyone who lives and believes in me, will never die."

This is taken from The Holy Bible, as noted in chapter *11,* verses 25 and *26* of St. John's Gospel. Brendan's birth date was *11-26!*

It was an incredibly profound moment for me, as I immediately made the connection! I felt a deep sense of hopefulness and looking back today, I realize God's compassionate love was infused into my heart at that very difficult moment, as I was guided to read this particular passage.

I believe Brendan wanted me to know at this crucial moment that everything would be alright in spite of the intense pain of separation I was experiencing. I don't know how much time had passed, but I remember feeling embraced by a warm and peaceful presence within and around me. I continued to reflect upon this chapter and verse over and over, almost mesmerized by its meaning and significance, and eventually, I fell into a deep and restful sleep.

Over the next few days, my husband and I made an appointment with a gentleman who could assist us with arrangements for a headstone. After discussing our options, we decided to have engraved in white, Gaelic lettering, the comforting words from Saint John, chapter 11,verses 25-26. I wanted the whole world to know that death isn't the end, but a new beginning, and that we pass on and see God face to face. We will see our loved ones again in a new life with our glorified bodies, and we will know one another! I know this for certain: Love never dies....Love is forever!

Since this passage alludes to the Resurrection, it is a common verse written on many Easter cards. As the years passed by, one Easter after another, I often read this very meaningful verse, believing this was Brendan's new birth date; his birth into new life.

Best to my recollection, my own birthday has never been on Easter Sunday, the "Feast of the Resurrection." Much to my surprise, just that did happen, on March 23, 2008! It was another one of life's uplifting blessings, I thought to myself. Then I smiled, as I "heard" Brendan say to me,

"Mom, you have a natural ability to make connections unlike anyone I know.......Happy Birthday!!" It was a truly awesome birthday gift I received, that year!

I believe everything is according to God's perfect plan. He knows when we will be born and when we will die.

"There is a time for everything, a season for every activity under heaven,
A time to be born and a time to die,
 A time to plant and a time to harvest.
A time to cry and a time to laugh,
A time to grieve and a time to dance"
(Ecclesiastes 3:1-2, 4).

The following beautifully written words, in the "textual footnote" of "The New Living Translation of The Holy Bible," significantly helped me to understand that God's love for us is insurmountable and that His plan for us is nothing less than perfect. It reads as follows:

"All of life is part of a well-orchestrated symphony for

which God has written the music. Thus we seek out God's plan for us, and we try to follow it with his guidance and direction."

For reasons unknown to us, the Lord had much greater plans for Brendan in the kingdom of heaven, as his mission on earth was completed.

Jesus said, "Do not let your hearts be troubled. Believe in God, believe also in me. In my Father's house, there are many dwelling places. If it were not so, would I have told you that I go and prepare a place for you? And if I go and prepare a place for you, I will come again and will take you to myself, so that where I am, there you may also be" (John 14:1-3).

This passage saturates my heart with peace, and fills me with the gift of hopefulness. The Lord's unconditional love for us is so great! We do not know the time God will take us home, but we do know that we will be called to that place he has faithfully prepared for us and our loved ones will be there to greet us.

Chapter 9 - Just a Breath Away

On September 27, 2003, there was a very important family wedding to attend. I asked myself, "How can I possibly go to a wedding? It's too soon!!" My heart was broken over the loss of my youngest son, Brendan, just sixteen days earlier. After a period of discernment, I eventually decided to attend the wedding with my husband, as I believed Brendan would have wanted us to attend. I had spoken to my cousin, Mary, who identified with that "intense pain of separation," since she, too, had lost her daughter in a car accident a few years earlier. On the day of the wedding, Mary phoned me to provide emotional support.

Then, on our drive to the wedding, I suddenly felt enlightened as I began to realize there was something very special about The Holy Ghost Church in Whitman, where the wedding was to take place. This was the same exact church at which my niece, Carrie, had gotten married just two years prior in August of 2001. I remembered the wonderful time we had at her wedding, with lots of dancing and laughter. My son, Brendan, and Carrie, were close in age and always had a special relationship. He once said she was everything he would like to find in a wife! He would often stop by her house on many occasions just to visit or bring a gift for her son, Stephen, who was also Brendan's god-son. Their relationship was indeed very special! I began to reflect upon the last time we were here at this church together and it was as if Brendan himself was reminding me of the significance of this place. I knew he was with me and I felt at ease; everything would be alright.

As my husband and I entered the church, I noticed the bride, Jill, had chosen red roses for her wedding bouquet and each of the groomsmen wore a rose boutonniere on his jacket. Red rose petals were scattered all along the carpet, carefully laid out for the bride. I remembered how Brendan always bought red roses for his girlfriend in celebration of their monthly anniversaries. The scent of roses seemed to fill the air and I felt Brendan's presence of peace and comfort.

As I glanced at the wedding program, my eyes caught

45

sight of a caption which read,

"In Remembrance," followed by these heartwarming words:

"We would also like to recognize our loved ones who are not able to be with us today. You are all sadly missed. Please remember, Brendan McGee…cousin of the groom."

I was overcome with emotion for the thoughtfulness of Peter and Jill. At the conclusion of the matrimonial celebration, the priest introduced them as husband and wife. As the happy couple made their way down the aisle, I noticed the rose petals dancing at their feet and beautiful music echoing throughout.

After congratulating the newlyweds, several of us were gathered together outside in front of the church. I was listening attentively to my Aunt Mary, who was speaking of how she couldn't sleep the night of Brendan's accident. Her heart was troubled and she knew something was wrong. The last thing she remembered was Brendan's loving embrace, as he bid her farewell, a few days before she was to return to her home in Florida. His final words were "It will probably be a long time until we see each other again." We continued our conversation and as we were talking, I *felt* someone walk up to me and *stand* at my side. I turned to look and no one was there. My husband's cousin, Betty, who stood directly across from me, said reassuringly, with words of confirmation and conviction,

"I felt him too!!"

We all stood in awe! Tears filled our eyes and we knew Brendan was definitely there!

About an hour later, as we gathered in the reception hall, Betty and I noticed there was an extra place setting at the table, beside where I was sitting. We looked at each other and smiled assuredly and agreed this one was for Brendan!

Next I knew, it was time for the "first dance" for the newlyweds. I remember I was standing by the table with my husband, and while thinking of Brendan, the words to "I Swear" began to play. I stood in awe as I listened intently to the beginning lyrics of the song…

"I swear by the moon and the stars in the sky, I'll be there.
And I swear like a shadow that's by your side, I'll be

there.

I see the questions in your eyes; I know what's weighing on your mind."

It was as if Brendan was speaking to me personally, as the words resonated in my heart, soul and mind. Only a couple hours had passed since we had the awesome, yet mysterious experience of feeling him walk right up to us. Then I glanced at the chair and place setting next to me, still unoccupied. The words to this song spoke to my heart so profoundly, and I knew that with the Grace of God and through Brendan's intervention, he was **still** standing by my side!

Chapter 10 - My Priceless Gift

There is a room in my house which I refer to as "Brendan's room." On the wall are photographs of cherished memories from the time he was a young baby until his adulthood. Included are captions of family gatherings celebrating birthdays, graduations, christenings, anniversaries, vacations, Easter, and Christmas to mention just a few! I thank God today I have so many treasured memories that I can reflect upon anytime I choose, as it brings me serenity and closure. This room is surely a sacred place for me to experience the quiet stillness anytime of the day or night.

About six months had passed since the loss of my son, Brendan, and I was by myself thinking of him. I was sitting on the floor looking through a desk drawer of Brendan's personal things and I came across a pair of his eyeglasses in a white envelope carefully marked, "FRAGILE." I took a deep breath, as I was overcome with emotion at finding them. I traced his handwriting across the envelope, as I pictured he had done so many months ago. Who would have ever known or thought it would come to this? Once again, I took a deep breath as I tried to regain my composure. I opened the envelope and tried them on; I could feel his gentle touch, a closeness that seemed so very near to me at that exact moment. I believe it was no mistake I found them on that particular day, as I will expound upon as this story unfolds. The frames fit my face perfectly. I took them off and carefully and reverently returned them to the envelope, assuming I would never wear them. However, Brendan had other plans for me, I would soon learn!

About a week earlier, I had my annual eye exam and was anticipating a call for when my glasses would be ready. On this particular day while I was at the cemetery, I stood in front of Brendan's stone and began to focus on his photograph mounted on the front. I was admiring how handsome he looked and how alive he seemed. As I spoke to him in the silence of my heart, I suddenly felt an indescribable burst of joy come over me! It was like Brendan was saying to me...

"Mom, look; I'm wearing the same glasses you tried on earlier this week! Remember how you thought you could never use them? How about bringing my glasses to the optometrist and ask to have them made into a pair of sunglasses for you?! By the way....HAPPY BIRTHDAY, MOM!!!!!"

My heart leaped for joy and I felt that unforgettable spiritual hug!!! It was all so timely. I had just had my eyes examined on my birthday and was told the glasses would be ready in approximately a week. I decided the sunglasses could be an add-on! I never imagined I would actually wear Brendan's glasses, let alone be a birthday gift from him!

Filled with excitement after our special "meeting of the minds," I drove home, picked up Brendan's glasses still sealed in the envelope where I had left them, and headed straight away to the optometrist's office! I was on a mission! I was greeted by the friendly receptionist who remembered Brendan, since he had received his glasses from this same office. She was more than happy to grant my request and thought it was a wonderful idea since Brendan's glasses had such great sentimental value. She remarked that it really wasn't an unusual request. It was an excellent way to honor his memory while using the glasses effectively. I was in my glory as I left the office that afternoon, looking forward to the day I would wear them.

Finally, the wonderful day arrived when I received a message that my new sunglasses were ready. I tried them on ....Ahhhh...A perfect fit, and how proud I was to wear them! It felt like Brendan was sharing in my joy! "Yes," I thought. "He's right here," and I couldn't keep from smiling! I left the office that day, and driving home, my heart was filled with gratitude and love for Brendan's inspirational guidance and direction.

Whenever sadness begins to saturate my heart, I eventually hear Brendan's gentle, comforting voice saying, "Where's your faith, Mom? Stay strong. It's going to be alright. Remember, I'm right here...I love you!"

Today, seven years later, I still wear proudly, "my priceless gift!"

Chapter 11 - Our Life is But a Mist

Each year on Memorial Day weekend, my husband and I look forward to an afternoon of planting spring flowers around our son Brendan's burial stone. We carefully turn the beds, prepare the soil and neatly arrange them in a decorative manner. I always feel Brendan is right there with us as I remember how much he enjoyed working outside in his own yard. I can still picture him so clearly, as if it was yesterday.

My husband knew he could always depend on Brendan to help, and this he truly missed after he was gone. Brendan also spent a couple summers working long hours grooming other peoples' yards while employed by a reputable landscaping company. Whatever he did, he always took great pride in his work!

Today, as I'm kneeling in the dirt, I'm picturing him and imagining myself asking the questions: "What do you think? How deep should I plant this? Does this look okay?" I know without a doubt that he is listening. I sense his loving presence, like a peacefulness I can't accurately describe; I just know he is close by. Then I take a few deep breaths and look up into the skies, as I ask for the strength to continue believing he is exceedingly happy and is "just beyond the horizon."

There we were on May 31, 2004, eight months and fifteen days since our family and friends gathered at this sacred place. The flowers were beautifully planted, perfectly to our satisfaction. My husband, Bob, and I stood and admired our work, knowing it would have met Brendan's approval! My husband gathered the shovels, rake and watering can to put in our special place where we keep our planting paraphernalia.

I remember kneeling on the ground, looking at my son's photo, which would soon be mounted on the front of the stone. I was still having trouble believing he was really gone and my eyes overflowed with tears. I kissed his very handsome face and combed his hair with my fingertips, wishing I had confiscated a few strands, back when I had the chance. Then I looked into his eyes and saw they were smiling back at me. Although I could not physically touch him, I knew that he was beside me in spirit.

A little later, I asked Bob to take a picture of me, as I gently brushed my hand over the memorial stone. I wanted to remember this very special day. It was 5:00 P.M.

Just before leaving the cemetery, as I was sitting in my car and staring at Brendan's memorial stone, I impulsively jumped out to take one more picture before Bob and I left. Now it was 5:02 P.M., as I noted the time on my camera. It has always been very important for me to keep all my treasured memoirs in photo albums, including dates and times, so that I can look back and reflect upon them, especially when I am missing Brendan and needing to remember these special moments.

A few days later, I brought my pictures to be developed. As I sat down and started to browse through them, I came across that one more picture I had taken and it almost took my breath away! In this picture, I saw *a fine, white, blanket of mist, likened to a waterfall, appearing to flow down from the sky, as it hovered over, and settled upon the upper part of Brendan's memorial stone.* I was in awe, as I held this photo reverently in my hands, and again, compared it to the photo taken just two minutes prior, which was devoid of this image.

I knew this photo had special significance in a seemingly "spiritual" way so I decided to have it enlarged and I placed it in an eight by ten picture frame! It became quite the conversation piece as friends and family members tried to make some sense out of it. Everyone had an opinion, but all agreed it was surely something unusual, mysterious and perhaps even "supernatural." Everyone looked upon it in awe.

A few months later while attending a prayer meeting, Karen, the facilitator of the group for that evening, opened a book entitled "Heaven, Your Real Home" and began to read the following words:

"Why, you do not even know what will happen tomorrow. What is your life? You are a *mist* that appears for a little while and then vanishes" (James 4:14).

I was in awe! This verse seemed to describe the above photograph perfectly and I was absolutely spellbound! Then when Karen mentioned the title of the book from which it came, I was even more awestruck. It seemed the Lord was speaking to me

51

personally and it brought tears to my eyes. I have always believed, heaven **is** our real home and where we will all be reunited one day. After the prayer meeting, I explained to Karen why I was so exhilarated over this particular verse she had read, as well as the profound significance of the book's title. This seemed to confirm what I already knew about *our real home* and I felt such an incredible peace about it.

I believe it was no coincidence she chose to bring this particular book to the prayer meeting that evening, and that she happened to open to the page containing the verse from James 4:14. As I have previously stated, there are no coincidences with God!! He is always faithful and always with me every hour of the day or night.

As a birthday gift to me, my niece, Kim, who was greatly impressed by this awe-inspiring photograph and the Scripture verse which described it so well, presented me with an enlargement, placed into a beautiful, silver, eight by ten picture frame, engraved as follows:

"What is your life? For you are a mist that appears for a little while and then vanishes" (James 4:14).

As I unwrapped the package, my eyes filled with tears and I had trouble finding the words to describe how very special this gift was to me. While looking at this amazing photograph, I immediately felt Brendan's presence and I was overcome with emotion. I gave Kim a big hug and tried to find the words to express my deep appreciation and thanks.

I believe if we just spend a few quiet moments every day with Jesus, remarkable things will happen. Since the loss of my son, I have spent many hours in front of the Blessed Sacrament and have received a peacefulness within my heart which is beyond my human understanding. The Lord says to me, "My grace is sufficient." Thankfully, I feel Brendan's presence all around me because he is always very near, within my heart, soul and mind.

As I wrote this chapter of my book, it was clear to me its title beautifully described what would become the front cover of my book, as it captures the true meaning of my belief in the beautiful promise of eternal life.

Chapter 12 - Vicki's Dream

At 9:30 in the morning of July 15, 2004, I received a phone call from my sister, Teresa, to tell me that our dad had passed away earlier that morning. My sister, Bernadette, and brothers, Paul and Blaise were all by his side, telling him *"it was okay to go,"* reassuring him they *"would take care of Mom,"* and also telling him how much they loved him.

The evening before, many of us were gathered together in his room. There he was, getting his necessary respiratory treatment, while still attempting to continue his humor by telling jokes. My mom had been there with him consistently for the past two days. Throughout the previous night, they had talked about their life together and their many blessings received over their nearly sixty years of a beautiful marriage. My mom will be forever grateful for having that very special time together with my dad as they had an opportunity to reminisce about so many tender moments and countless cherished memories.

Having been awake most of the previous night, my mom went to take a short nap. About an hour later, being concerned she hadn't returned, my dad began asking repeatedly, "Did someone wake up mom?" It was obvious he wanted her to be there with him; this will always be a most clear and precious memory of mine.

That evening, before he fell asleep, my mom and several of my siblings, circled around his bed, and prayed with him. He looked so peaceful.

Later, I sat at his bedside for at least an hour as I watched him sleep, assisted by an oxygen mask, fitted snugly on his face. How I loved my dad: a thoughtful, compassionate, totally caring, faith-filled man! The last thing I did for him was wash his dentures and place them on the shelf at his bedside, as he had asked me to do. I can still hear his voice, as I recall his last words to me, "You can leave them over there and the nurse will get them for me in the morning."

I told my husband I planned to come back and spend the following night with him. I also remember speaking to my nurse manager, telling her my dad seemed much better and I could come to work the next morning. Little did I know, everything would change.

When I received the phone call from my sister, Teresa, and heard the words, *"Dad passed away this morning,"* I was caught off guard. I had trouble accepting what was being said, but at the same time, I was so grateful for the endearing moments we had spent the evening before. I had thought he seemed better, but I know now that God allowed that special interval of time for all his family to be with him, and to lavish him with all the love we had yet to give.

My next thought was to call Vicki, my son, Brendan's former fiancée. Since the tragic loss of our son, she continued to stay in touch with us and I knew she would want to know. As I began to tell her, she quickly interrupted me as she said:

"You don't have to tell me; I already know; Brendan's Grampa passed away this morning, didn't he?" She then began to share with me, her dream. She spoke of how she was really missing Brendan and thinking about him all the time. She asked him if he would come to her in a dream. Then, on this particular morning, she did in fact, have that dream, and began to explain:

"In my dream, there he was, all dressed up, looking so handsome. It was so wonderful to see him again. We talked for a while and then he told me 'had to go,' but I couldn't go with him."

She continued telling me about her dream and explained that Brendan was wearing a backpack over his shoulders! She wanted to ask him where he was going with this backpack. However, he seemed in a hurry as he went through a doorway, headed down a lighted hallway and disappeared into a fog. Eventually, she lost sight of him. Next in her dream, she remembers asking a lady in white if she could chase after him to let him know he was wearing a backpack. Minutes later, the lady in white returned and said she couldn't catch him. Then Vicki said she woke up, went downstairs, and told her mom that Brendan's Grampa just passed away and Brendan went to meet him.

All the while Vicki was talking, I just stood there at the other end of the receiver, trying to absorb what she was saying. As

54

she was telling me about her dream of Brendan going to meet my dad, it seemed like a fairytale. It was like "heavenly music" to my ears; what a beautiful thing! Between my sobs, I tried to thank her, but I couldn't find the words to express my sincere gratitude. Perhaps she will never know just how much I needed to hear her story and I will be forever grateful to her for sharing it with me that morning.

Later, I listened to **these words**, which were spoken by my dad at the moment of his passing, from my sister, Bernadette, who was with him during his last hours. While choking back the tears, she said to me,

"Just before dad took his last breath, he looked up and said, '*I can't go this way.*' We kept telling him, it's okay, it's okay, it's okay to go, we love you, we love you, we'll take care of Mom."

I believe with all my heart that Brendan ran to my dad's side at that exact moment and said, "I'm right here, Grampa!"

Vicki's dream occurred at approximately 8:00 in the morning; my dad had passed away at 7:20 that same morning. I felt shivers go up and down my spine! What an incredible dream!

And what an emotional meeting it must have been for them! As I visualized Brendan and my dad together, embraced in each other's arms, I felt in my heart everything would be okay because they were together now; my dad was safely home! Clearly, I knew that my son, Brendan, and my dad were reunited and walking together in the heights of heaven. I cried and cried and cried…tears of joy for both of them, tears of sorrow, tears of missing my son, and tears of thanks to Vicki for relaying this incredible dream to me. Knowing they are together brings me an abundance of peace, serenity, and lasting hope. I thank God that I believe, and I know that we will all be together one day, for all eternity, forever in the company of Jesus, the angels and all the saints!

The following poem was printed on a small card and carefully placed by Brendan's memorial stone. This captures one of the more beautiful definitions of love.

The poem reads:

So what is love?
If thou wouldst know
The heart alone can tell:
Two minds with but a single thought,
Two hearts that beat as one.
And whence comes love?
Like morning bright
Love comes without thy call.
And how dies love?
A spirit bright,
Love never dies at all.

Three years later, on August 21, 2007, we received an unexpected phone call from Vicki, wanting to talk to us. It was a tender moment as she arrived at the front door. It was so good to see her, for it had been a long while. She wanted to let my husband and I know she had met someone and had accepted his proposal of marriage. Both of us were very happy she had found someone who brought joy and fulfillment back into her life. We gave her a big hug and wished her the very best.

Just a couple hours later, as I was driving along interstate 195, coming off the exit not far from where Brendan's accident had occurred, I saw the most gorgeous rainbow in the sky! It almost took my breath away and immediately I thought of Brendan, and what Vicki had said to me that day. I felt very inspired to phone her and tell her about the rainbow. I felt very strongly it was a sign from Brendan giving her his blessing! She was glad I called, and thanked me for sharing my thoughts with her. In June of 2008, my husband and I were honored to attend her wedding.

Chapter 13 - Just Around the Corner

It was early in the evening, and my youngest sister, Cecelia and her thirteen year old daughter, Danielle, were visiting with my mom. The quiet stillness in the house spoke aloud of my dad's absence. A thought crosses my mind as I write this story, that perhaps he knew this…As this story unfolds, it will speak for itself.

My parents had a content marriage for sixty years. As they shared similar interests, it was rare to ever see one without the other. It was in this comfortable home they had spent their last seventeen, peaceful years together. Interestingly, this was from *July* of the year 1987, until *July* of 2004.

Sitting at the dining room table, Cecelia and Danielle were busy helping my mom complete the many notes of thanks and appreciation to several caring and thoughtful friends and family members who had sent cards of sympathy and love since his death, just a week earlier. All the while, they were reflecting upon the genuine love our dad had always shared throughout his lifetime with everyone he had met.

Danielle had left the room a few minutes earlier and now was returning to rejoin her mom and grandmother in a game of scrabble. As she entered the room, she stopped short in her tracks, obviously stunned and unprepared for what she was about to see. Her jaw dropped and her mouth opened widely. She appeared dazed and speechless as her eyes were glued upon what she clearly saw across the opposite side of the room. The look on her amazed face spoke volumes! She later sat with me and described her experience in detail. I listened intently to these words:

"I was walking into the room and I saw a white shadow in front of the bedroom doorway. It was near the holy water font, hanging on the wall. Then I saw Grampa's face. It was glowing. Then I saw all white again, but I didn't see his face anymore. It happened so fast, like when you blink, you see a flash in your eyes and then it's gone again. I was scared at first and wondered why he chose me. Later, I felt really honored that I got to see him and that he came to me!"

Meanwhile, my mother had remarked, "For as far back as I can remember, this holy water font has been hanging on this wall," alluding to the area where Danielle had seen her Grampa's face. Then, with tears in her eyes, she began to reminisce about how my dad would stand in that very spot as he said goodnight to her before going into his bedroom that was set up with the necessary oxygen equipment. He was always considerate of my mother's needs and he didn't want to disturb her night's rest.

My mom, like myself, believes without a doubt, he *is* right here, keeping her company every day until we will meet again and be together for eternity. For the reader who is still skeptical, believe that we believe, and hopefully, one day you also will have a profound experience to hold within your own heart.

Less than two weeks later, my niece, Danielle, had another unusual, yet exciting experience. Her parents had gone out to dinner to celebrate their wedding anniversary and she was home watching her two younger brothers. Danielle and her best friend were downstairs in the playroom looking at some music videos on her computer. She explained to me what had occurred that evening…

"I happened to look up at the clock near my computer, where my friend and I were sitting, and it was 7:11 P.M. Ironically, July 11th is my parents' anniversary date. A couple minutes later, when I glanced again, it was 7:15 P.M. Ironically again, July 15th was the date Grampa passed away. I began to think, is this all coincidental? Then, the next time I glanced at the clock, it was 7:25 P.M., and that's when I knew it wasn't just a coincidence….that's when I really knew, it meant something special because July 25th is Grampa's birthday! Not being able to keep this to myself any longer, I decided to tell my girlfriend, sitting next to me. Then, no sooner did the words come out of my mouth, when I heard a noise over by the stairway. I looked, assuming it was Thomas or Matthew coming to say goodnight. That's when I saw a *flash of white* going by the front of the staircase. It went by quickly, but I knew it was Grampa. I said to my friend, 'My Grampa's here!' This time, I wasn't scared at all. I knew it was him and I felt really good!''

This story wouldn't be complete if I didn't include what

occurred at my brother Paul's home in North Carolina about six months after my dad passed. My sister-in-law, Suzie, sat up in bed one morning and saw a strange image that looked like my father. At first, she thought she was dreaming, but seconds later, she saw my father sitting in a chair, across the hall, in her living room. Immediately, she tried to awake her husband, Paul (my brother). By this time, the image of my father had vanished. Ironically, this was the same chair he sat in opening Christmas presents the previous year!

Evidently, my dad didn't feel his mission was completed because Suzie called to tell me he "visited" again, approximately one month later. As I listened attentively to her voice on the other end of the receiver, I could almost see her face as she began to explain...

"I saw your dad again!! Paul was outside working in the garden, and I was in the kitchen washing dishes. I thought Paul had come inside because I sensed someone behind me in the living room and your dad was sitting in that same chair again! Completely startled and caught off guard, I ran to the door and yelled for Paul to come in!! When I came back inside, it was too late. He wasn't there anymore. Paul wondered why he makes appearances for me and not him, but I didn't know what to tell him."

About a year later, my husband and I went to visit my brother, Paul, and his wife, Suzie. The first thing I wanted to do was to sit down in that same chair where our dad had sat and where he loved to relax. My brother walked me into his living room and said, "This is it!" I sat down, closed my eyes and visualized our dad's smiling face and I could almost hear him say, "I'm right here!"

Then, we all began to reminisce, as we often did whenever we got together. Our dad truly loved his family get-togethers. My husband, Bob, and I began to talk to Paul and Suzie about our dad's visits to our home in Rochester during the period of time our house was being built. "He knew he was welcome anytime," my husband commented. "I remember it so well. Your dad and I would walk around our yard which he called The McGee Estate and jokingly he would count the number of available campsites!"

He was certainly one of a kind, deeply loved, respected and admired; we proudly called him …our wonderful dad! We truly miss him and his smiling face, as he was always ready with another "Leo joke!" Certainly, he will continue living in the hearts of all his thirteen children until we see him again when we are called to our home in heaven, where there will be no more sorrow, no more sickness, and no more pain. Oh, what joy there will be!! And we will all say together, our voices in unison…"He's right here!!!"

On Christmas night, 2010, I was sitting with my niece Lori, who I hadn't seen for about three years. Lori and her husband, Dave, were home for the holidays and there we were, catching up on all the news. It was so wonderful to see her and to have the opportunity to spend some quality time together. We began to talk about my book, as she read the first couple pages of this story. Tears filled her eyes…

"Don't mind me; I'm so emotional"….

I gave her a hug and said, "Aren't we all, especially at this time of year?"

Then she asked me if I remembered giving her a silver colored pendant at Brendan's wake. I had a vague recollection as she began to describe what it looked like, but I really couldn't remember much about it at all. As we sat together on the divan in the living room, she began to tell me about her very moving experience.

"At Brendan's funeral, I received a pendant from you. It was a silver color and oval in shape. On one side, there was a man, presumably a saint. I'm not sure if I got this at the actual funeral or at the wake the night before. Nonetheless, I immediately put it in my purse in a zippered pocket. When I returned to San Antonio I changed the purse I had carried with me back home. As I was emptying its contents and transferring everything to the other purse, I realized I could no longer find the pendant in the pocket in which I placed it. This, of course, was upsetting. I looked everywhere I could think of, but to no avail! It was gone!! A few days later, I think the reality and finality of Brendan's death hit me. The pain felt like a punch to the gut and never in the years since I had moved from home did I feel more alone. I felt every single mile between myself and everyone else who held Brendan's memories dear. I called my mother and she did her best to comfort me, but it was hard living so far away. I was still pretty upset when I got off the phone. I lay down on my couch crying, until I felt a *strong sense of comfort*. I looked up and in the middle of the couch cushion was the pendant! I had been home for days and had been sitting on this couch for hours, but I had not seen the pendant before this moment. It was that *sense of comfort,* and I just knew I wasn't alone. I *felt* Brendan's strong presence. He was... *right there!*"

All I could say to Lori, was "I'm so glad we had this time together, and that you shared this beautiful story with me. Just as you felt Brendan's loving, comforting presence close by your side, we both know who put the pendant there on the couch! We don't understand *how*, but we know beyond a shadow of a doubt, it was Brendan and that was certain. He *is* right here trying to help us any way he can. Thank you so much Lori, for sharing this very moving story with me. I love you."

As this story continues, I feel it is very appropriate to include another, which is both heartwarming and comforting, and will especially apply to a young mom whose baby is born just a month or two after the passing of someone they love dearly. As written earlier in this book, my niece, Carrie, and my son, Brendan, were always very close. This is the story of another spiritual encounter with Brendan. Carrie explained,

"I remember it all so well because it was at Stephen's birthday party, just one month after his godfather, Uncle Brendan had passed away. I was missing him a lot and I knew Stephen was missing him too. Brendan was always there with something special for Stephen at every one of his birthday parties. I was trying to settle my son, Aidan, and after about half an hour, he finally closed his eyes and was on his way to sleep. Then, I lay down beside him, with my head gently upon his pillow. As I was lying there, I heard the bedroom door opening ever so quietly. I jumped up, and there, standing in the doorway, I *saw* Brendan! I know it was Brendan. He was wearing a white tee shirt, jeans, and his work boots as he usually wore when he stopped by after work or on his way to school. I didn't see his face but I *know* it was him! It was his shape and I *felt* him. It was at that moment I realized he had probably been there the whole time, helping me calm Aidan. I often had a tough time settling him at bedtime. It was always a challenge to get him to fall asleep, and Brendan knew this! When I heard the bedroom door open, I believe it was Brendan trying to *leave the room, not to enter it!* I will never forget that night, and I will never forget what I saw! Thank you so much, Aunt Maggie, for believing in me and for including this treasured memory in your book! What an awesome gift!! *Yes, indeed...he is, right here!*"

I am convinced, our loved ones are all around us in another dimension, just around the corner from us. Now and again, they become visible to us, through our own special God-given gifts, according to His plan for us. For some, it is a gift of spiritual vision. For others, it is an awareness of a presence in some form or another that speaks deep within our soul and *we know that we know.* Oftentimes, we intuitively receive a message, some more subtle than others, and it's always very clear that by our side...He's right here!!

Chapter 14 - Yellow Roses From Heaven

During Mass one morning, my mom noticed a lovely, yellow rose at the end of the pew where she was sitting. She thought it was odd that it was there and thought that the person who left the rose would probably return after realizing it had been left behind. Eventually, a woman did come to claim "the mysterious rose." She was very grateful that she had recovered it and off she went.

Later that afternoon, my mom went for a walk along the roads near her home. For some reason, she decided to take an alternate route, for a different, yet pleasant change of scenery. As she walked, her eyes caught sight of something on the side of the road a short distance ahead. As she walked closer, she was stunned at what she saw!

In a little pile, there was a bunch of beautiful, fresh, yellow roses, laying on the ground! She was totally amazed at what she saw! Where had they come from? It really made absolutely no sense at all! She stopped to pick them up, still dumbfounded as to where they came from.

She began to think about her husband, of nearly sixty years until the Lord had called him home on July 15, 2004, which was only about a month prior to this date. Over the years past, the two of them often took walks together, but on this day, she was especially missing him and feeling his absence.

They had also done a lot of traveling together after we all left home and began to have families of our own. I often hear my mom reminisce about their visits to The Holy Land and Portugal, where they visited the shrine of Our Lady of Fatima, as well as their several visits to England, where my parents first met.

My mom's favorite flowers are yellow roses. She began to remember the first time my dad bought them for her, as she recollected we were on vacation at Parkwood Beach in Wareham. My parents rented a cottage for a couple weeks every summer and I still recall my siblings and I being so excited about vacationing together. My dad had to work during the first week, so had to commute quite a distance from Brockton, when the only access was "the old Cape highway." On the second week, he surprised her with an absolutely gorgeous bouquet of beautiful, yellow roses!

"This was a rare occasion," she said, "since yellow roses were quite expensive back then and we really couldn't afford them, so it was certainly unexpected!"

I'm sure it pleased my dad immensely to be able to buy them for her! He was such a wonderful, caring, generous man, and he loved my mom unconditionally, as she did him. My parents were such a powerful example to our family of thirteen children.

We will probably never know from *where* the yellow roses came, but somehow, we know from *whom*! It never ceases to amaze me how the Lord provides us with these special, yet utterly, mysterious events to help us feel somehow connected with those we love and miss and think about at any given time of the night or day.

Chapter 15 - A Miracle of Love

This remarkable story is one I am especially happy to share with anyone who reads this book. It is about two people who pledged their love for each other on August 19, 1944. My parents did everything together and they never had any secrets between them. Whenever anyone asked my mom how she and my dad managed to raise eight girls and five boys, her answer was always the same: "By the grace of the Sacrament of Matrimony!" It was a powerful example of the belief that marriage takes three, with God in the center. Tenderly pulling at my heartstrings, is the memory of a dream Brendan's fiancée had of Brendan going to meet my dad on the morning of his death. Over the past several weeks, I've been gathering my thoughts to write about this fascinating story I believe will touch many hearts. As I sat in front of the Blessed Sacrament after morning Mass, I felt very inspired to begin writing this story, at a time when I particularly sensed a "closeness to heaven" and to those who have entered its gates to be with Jesus and Mary.

On July 15, 2004, at seven twenty in the morning, my dad went to God, as he was lovingly surrounded by my brothers, Paul and Blaise, and sister, Bernadette. They had all stayed with him throughout the entire night. In a previous story, I described in greater detail, the warm-heartening, tender moments we spent as a family together the evening before. I tearfully remember several of us children, as well as our mom encircling his bed and praying with him at the end of the evening. He had been anointed with the Sacrament of the Sick, and had received the Eucharist the day before, so I knew he was at peace. Then, what a special blessing, and how fitting it was, to have his daughter, Bernadette, at his bedside throughout the night, caring for him as his own special nurse. My dad was always so proud of her and they definitely had a special bond as he did with all of us. We were truly blessed with a dad who exhibited love, compassion, understanding, honesty, and other self-giving qualities, too numerous to mention. We all miss him very much, but we know and believe he's right here!

As mentioned in another story of this book, my mom is a spirit-filled woman and a true believer of God's love and mercy. She has always been devoted to her prayer life; For example, for many years, she arrived a half hour early before daily Mass to lead a group of parishioners in the recitation of the rosary. Until recently, due to her age of eighty-nine years and decreased agility, she has not been able to attend morning Mass, as was her routine for many years. My dad also accompanied her to daily Mass and the rosary until the age of eighty-three when he was unable due to health reasons. My dad loved the Lord and had a special devotion to our Blessed Mother; he carried a holy card of Mary in his wallet, which I never knew until after he had passed on.

In August of the year 1990, my parents were in York, England, celebrating their 45th wedding anniversary. My mom was born and raised in Norwich, England and my dad met and married her during the war. They were always very happy to return for a visit to England whenever they could, which they did several times over the years. On this special day on the 13th of August, my dad bought her a beautiful, gold chain necklace, a gift my mom treasured with all her heart. Little did they know, this interesting story about this necklace would unfold several years later.

In September of 2004, my mom's younger brother, Dennis, was very ill and she and I planned a visit to see him. Sadly, we didn't have my dad to accompany us, but somehow both my mom and I knew that he probably *was* with us in spirit.

He loved going to England! As a matter of fact, as he was being wheeled on a stretcher to the elevator to be transferred to Mount Sinai Hospital, I clearly remember he said to us with a big smile on his face, "I'd like to go to England!" I said to him, "You can go anywhere you'd like, Dad!!" God bless him! I remember that moment like it was yesterday. Tucked within the confines of my heart are memories of my dad, who was always ready to tell a joke every chance he got, bringing joy to wherever he went. Even if his joke wasn't so funny, we still called it a "Leo joke" and laughed anyway. He loved telling a joke to a person who appeared a bit cranky, hoping it would cheer him up, which it usually did! A favorite one of his jokes was when he pretended to kill a mosquito in the middle of the winter and he would have the fellow believing he actually had seen one! How we miss him so very much.

One morning during our visit with my aunt and uncle, my mom realized the beautiful, gold chain necklace she had placed around her neck earlier that morning was missing! This necklace was obviously very precious to her, as it was a very special anniversary gift from my dad. Her heart sank! She prayed to Saint Anthony, the patron saint of lost articles. She searched diligently. We looked in every possible hole and corner without success. It was so terribly upsetting and we knew we were hopelessly defeated. Eventually, my mom concluded the Lord was trying to teach her "detachment," and decided to try to accept her loss.

Sixteen months later on January 2nd, 2006, exactly one week before her birthday, my mom was at Saint Peter's Church attending morning Mass. She had arrived one half hour earlier to say the rosary and join with those present as she had done for many years. Upon returning her rosary beads to her pocketbook, which she had placed on the bench at her side, she noticed a rolled up, tangled, gold chain, lying in a heap on the closed zipper of her pocketbook. Quite bewildered, yet not realizing what it actually was, she put it into her pocket, and would examine it more closely after she got home since Mass was about to begin. It never occurred to her that it might be the missing necklace she had lost in England! I guess she had resigned to the fact it was gone for good and had accepted the "lesson of detachment."

After my mom arrived home, she took this crinkled up, tangled, gold chain out of her pocket and began to look at it more closely, while carefully untangling it. As she laid the untangled, gold chain necklace across her kitchen table, she realized it was the necklace she had lost sixteen months prior. It was the *exact* same gold chain necklace my Dad had bought for her on that memorable day they spent in York, England! Completely amazed and in awe, she called me on the phone to tell me about this very mysterious "return" of her necklace! She also remarked how she had bought a new pocketbook since the visit to England, so she knew the necklace wasn't somehow stuck in the lining, since it wasn't the same one.

After conversing about it, we came to the conclusion we will never really know how this necklace, lost somewhere across the ocean a year and four months earlier, mysteriously reappeared on top of her pocketbook, which she had zippered shut just twenty minutes earlier!! We can only speculate or theorize about the possible answers. All we knew for definite, was the gold chain was lost and now was found or recovered somehow by an "unknown source." My mom thought that it was perhaps Saint Anthony, or her husband (my dad), or possibly her brother, Dennis, who had passed away on February 8, 2005. Then we chuckled and thought about the possibility of my dad and my uncle getting together and bringing my mom an early birthday gift, just one week before the 9th of January!

For what it's worth, I believe it was my dad saying "I love you" to my mom, "now and forever until we meet again. Until then, wear this necklace as a sign of my undying love for you and please don't lose it again," as he brushed his finger across her nose, something of special meaning to them.

My parents' sixtieth wedding anniversary was just one month and four days after my dad's death. I can almost hear him saying to my mom…"It took me sixteen months to bring my gift to you for our sixtieth wedding anniversary! The Lord keeps me very busy here, praying for all of you. Please keep praying for me…Love Always, Dad. P.S. I'm right here!"

We both agree on this: Never underestimate the power of prayer!!

Chapter 16 - The Purple Flower Story

One mid-afternoon during the first week of May in 2005, I was thinking about Brendan and missing him, since it was nearing Mother's Day. It had been a year and eight months since his passing. Earlier in the week, I sat down and read the cards he had given me over the years -- so many memories. I actually had set a few of them out and pretended he had just given them to me. It was my way of trying to cope with the terrible loss I was feeling, and in the deepest crevices of my heart, I felt connected to him. On this particular day, as I drove into the parking lot of an outdoor mall, I felt his presence very strongly and I "heard" him say to me, "Happy Mother's Day, Mom," as his voice whispered to my heart. I can't recall a single Mother's Day when he didn't present me with a gift, one which always had significant and special meaning.

Inadvertently, I drove towards the garden center and caught sight of a particular plant set upon the ground, amongst several others. For some reason which I cannot explain, I was inspired to drive closer, as I set my gaze upon an ordinary purple petunia plant. I felt as though I was having a private conversation with Brendan and he was directing me to this particular plant saying, "This one is for you, Mom!" I kept all this to myself, sort of a special thing between us and I felt him right there with me as a passenger in my car. I walked into the store with the potted plant and asked the gentleman at the cash register if I could leave it there until my return, to which he graciously consented. Then I hurried through the store to complete my shopping. All the while, I pondered silently about the petunia plant Brendan had just "bought" for me. This all put a silly smile on my face as I felt his love totally fill my heart. I could almost visualize him having a friendly conversation with the gentleman at the cash register until my return.

Having found those items I originally planned to buy, I was now ready to check out. I thanked the gentleman for holding the plant for me and very soon, I was placing the plant securely on the passenger seat. Upon my arrival home, I decided to place the petunia plant at my front door. We had had a week of cool, misty weather, and although I had planned to bring it to the cemetery, I decided to leave it where it was. A few days went by and with the help of the sun's rays filtering through the clouds, it was growing into a beautiful, flowering, purple petunia plant! I just kept admiring it and thanking Brendan, remembering his thoughtful ways. This continued to be "our little secret," which helped me so much during this very special time of the year.

On the evening of May 22, 2005, my husband, Bob, and I went out for a walk. He noticed the blooming petunia plant at our front door and asked me if I still planned to bring it to the cemetery, as was my original intention. Since the plant had grown so much and was too heavy for the plant hanger, I decided to leave it on our front deck for all to see and enjoy.

The next evening on the 23rd of May, I attended a prayer meeting at Sacred Heart Catholic Church in Middleboro, Massachusetts, where about six or seven of us gathered. In quiet meditation before the Blessed Sacrament, we listened to music, accompanied by lyrics which spoke words of solace and comfort. I felt a sense of peace, thinking of Brendan, knowing he was spiritually present.

After an hour or so had passed, one of the girls who I see only at the prayer meetings, said to me, "I don't want you to think I'm crazy or anything…I wasn't going to say anything, but my praying was being interrupted by this very persistent voice. I think it's your son, saying to me, *'Tell my mother I love her,'* and again very persistently, *'Tell my mother I love her…..and I love the purple flowers.'* Does this mean anything to you?"

I looked at her in awe as tears filled my eyes. I was utterly speechless! All I could say while stumbling over my words was, "Oh my God!" I was dumbfounded! She had no knowledge of the "encounter" with my son, at the garden center a couple weeks earlier. She also had never met Brendan, but knew he had died since I had poured my heart out to this prayer group many months earlier when I was desperate for answers. All I could do was hug and thank her for the gift she was given, to deliver to me this message of healing.

I will be forever grateful that she relayed this incredibly powerful message to me from my son on that evening. I realize not everything is explainable in logical terms, but I do believe Brendan is always available to us, just the other side of a prayer. One thing I know also is that God is always faithful and He doesn't give us more than we can handle, when we place our trust in Him. He is a God of many surprises and promises.

Very interestingly, five years later, on Mother's Day, 2010, my daughter, Lisa, received an adorable, seven week old kitten, which her sons, Vincent and Nicholas named, Petunia!! Luke, who is two and one-half years old, calls her, "Tuna!"

I continue to thank the Lord every day for the many gifts bestowed upon me, including my family, faith, health and His constant protection for all those I love.

Vincent   Brendan   Nicholas

Chapter 17 - You're Not Like Me Yet

It was June 15, 2005, just one year and nine months after the passing of my son, Brendan. Whenever I was feeling very sad and missing him, and in much need of a mental uplift, spending time with my grandchildren always filled my heart with an amazing comfort. And so it was, especially on this particular day, which I had spent with two of my precious grandchildren, Vincent, age six and Nicholas, age two.

At eight o'clock in the evening, as I was driving my grandchildren home, I had no idea what was about to transpire! My two year old grandson, Nicholas, was asleep in his car seat, so it gave Vincent and me a chance for some quiet and reflective moments together, ones which we always cherished. We began to have a conversation about our enjoyable day. I thanked him for the time we spent together and stated I was glad he was beginning to feel better. (Vincent had woken up that morning with a sore throat). A minute or two later, Vincent began to tell me about an incredible experience he had encountered very early in the morning of that same day, an experience which will undoubtedly pull at your heartstrings, as it did mine…..Spoken verbatim from the mouth of a six year old child, were these words….

…. "Gramma, I saw Uncle Brendan this morning."

I asked him, "You saw little Brendan this morning?" (Little Brendan is Vincent's cousin).

He answered, "No, I saw *Uncle* Brendan!"

Then he began to explain:

"It was early in the morning…Everyone was sleeping. I could hear the birds singing, but it was still dark outside. I was thinking of Uncle Brendan and wishing I could talk to him like I always used to do, and I was asking him to help me to feel better because my throat was really hurting me and I felt really bad. Then I heard him say, *'Open your eyes,'* so I opened my eyes and there him was!! It's really funny because he already died and you can't die again, but he was standing right there beside my bed. It's like if you kill a fly, it can't die anymore. Uncle Brendan can't die anymore either!!"

What an amazing analogy, I thought to myself and I continued to listen intently. I wanted to hear everything he had to say.

Then Vincent exclaimed, "And Gramma….he wasn't wearing his glasses!"

At this point, I explained to him, "Uncle Brendan's eyes are perfect now, so he doesn't need them anymore."

Vincent continued:

"I thought he was going to cry, so I went to give him a hug, and my hand went right through him!"

Trying not to overreact, I interrupted and asked him, …"Were you scared?"

Vincent quickly responded…. "Gramma, it was Uncle Brendan!! And he was wearing his favorite orange tank top. Then Uncle Brendan said, *'It's okay; you're not like me yet, but one day you will be.'* He told me he really misses me and he loves me so much. I told him I really, really miss him too! He told me he will *always* be with me, and I can *always* talk to him anytime I want. And he said he hopes I feel better."

Vincent's Uncle Brendan had spent the evening of September 11, 2003, visiting with him and his cousins at my

73

daughter's home, and that was the last time they had been together, before the accident occurred. Also, on that same night, Brendan had bought a birthday present for Vincent, who would be five years old on the seventeenth of September. His Uncle Brendan had bought him a pair of "Batman pajamas," just as he had requested. However, it was not until after the accident, that we found the gift somewhere in the back of the crushed vehicle. Vincent loved the birthday present from his Uncle Brendan. About a week later, he wrote a thank you note on a wooden board, that he and his cousin built, and brought it to the cemetery where it still remains, standing up against a special tree nearby.

I gently suggested to Vincent that perhaps his Uncle Brendan knew how much he wanted to talk to him. Then, with a smile on his face, he nodded his head, and said with confidence and assurance in his voice,

" I didn't get to see *him,* so he came to see *me!*"

Overcome with emotion, I said to him, "If Uncle Brendan comes to you again, will you please tell him for me, that I love him so very much and I'm so glad he came to you!?"

Vincent shook his head, agreeing that he would. Then I began to explain how very special he must be to his uncle, and Vincent just continued to smile.

I will certainly remember this conversation with Vincent forever, and these words will remain a part of me, deeply ingrained into the fiber of my being!

On this memorable evening, a year and nine months after Brendan's passing, I believe there was finally some closure for Vincent.

We sat and talked for a little while longer. I asked him if he had told anyone else, and he tenderly answered… "No… just you." I felt so blessed that he had chosen me to listen to this incredible and heartwarming story.

After I left Vincent and Nicholas that evening, I sat in my car and closed my eyes, while trying to absorb what Vincent had told me. This conversation with Vincent was such an incredibly emotional experience for me and I was so happy for him. I also felt very close to Brendan. All I could do was sit there and thank him for all he had done for Vincent, not that I understood any of it! I just knew that it did, in fact, happen.

Later on, when I spoke to my daughter about what Vincent had shared with me, she confirmed that he had come downstairs at about 3:30 that morning, and eventually fell asleep on the couch. She kept him home from school because he wasn't feeling well. Then he spent the day with me, since his mom was working.

Later that night and the next day, it was all I could think about; I felt such peace! I continued to reflect and meditate upon all that had transpired and to absorb into the depths of my soul what Vincent had shared with me.

Children are so special in the eyes of God. I believe Vincent was given a gift to intervene for me, to open my eyes, so I could see through his and gain a new vision or insight. As a grieving mother, I was incapable of having this experience myself, because I was blocked by an emotional fog. However, Vincent's intelligence, perceptiveness, and sensitivity enabled him to have this incredible experience, which brought me a consolation beyond words and a birth of new hope.

Just as importantly, Vincent was able to process his own grief according to his own understanding and receive the closure he needed to bring him healing, comfort and hope. I believe it also helped him to gain a new confidence and sense of self-worth. Vincent knows we will all be together one day in heaven. I am so grateful he had the freedom to talk to me when he was ready, and the time and place was provided for him.

I owe it all to the healing touch of God through a little child. What comes to my mind is a Bible verse quoted from Matthew, chapter 19 verses 14-15, which says:

Jesus said, "Let the little children come to me, and do not prevent them. For of such is the kingdom of heaven. And he put his hands on their heads and blessed them before he left."

A few days later, while we stopped at the cemetery to pay a visit to his Uncle Brendan, Vincent said, "I have an angel in heaven I can talk to anytime I want!"

His cousin, Brendan, standing beside him said, "Me too!" (See chapter 3, entitled Little Did We Know).

Vincent and Brendan are only five months apart in age, and I often hear them, as they share their stories about their uncle.

They seem to find comfort in one another as they reminisce about all the special times they had with their Uncle Brendan.

I recently came across the lyrics of the song "I Shall Be Like Him" (When I Shall Reach The More) written by W. A. Spencer, a Christian musician, and my heart skipped a beat as the words jumped off the page. As I read the lyrics, I knew in my heart, Brendan is one with Jesus in the glory of heaven; the words mimicked what Vincent heard his Uncle Brendan say to him, "You're not like me yet."

After I wrote this chapter of my book, it was Vincent who decided upon its title, and of equal importance to me, this brought an abundance of joy to my heart. There are no coincidences with God!

Looking through the journals I had written over the years past, I saw that I had placed a bright red asterisk next to a Bible verse I had read in one of my daily meditation books from May 18, 2008. "Beloved, we are the children of God now; what we shall be has not yet appeared. We do know that when he appears, *we shall be like him*" (1 John 3:2).

On the evening I first read this verse, I had no idea I would be writing a book just two years later. Seemingly, the Lord continued revealing to me words of Scripture that affected me in a special and profound way, to be included in this story. As the Light of The Holy Spirit shone upon me and opened the eyes of my soul from deep within, I felt very inspired to follow the dictates of my heart.

In closing, I write and reflect upon these words, taken from Proverbs, chapter 3, verses 5-6.

"Trust in the Lord with all thine heart, and lean not unto thine own understanding. In all thy ways acknowledge Him, and He will direct thy paths."

Chapter 18 - A Welcomed Visitor

On November 29, 2006, three years after our son passed away, and just three days after he would have been thirty one, my husband, Bob, and I had a most incredible experience! I had agreed to be on call for work starting at three o'clock in the morning. After questioning myself why I agreed to such a thing, I decided to lie down and get some rest.

Before falling asleep, I read a prayer card I had received three years earlier. For the first time, I was able to read and reflect upon the following words:

"Death is nothing at all. I have only slipped away into the next room. I am I, and you are you. Whatever we were to each other, that we still are. Call me by my old familiar name; speak to me in the easy way which you always used. Put no difference in your tone, wear no forced air of solemnity or sorrow. Laugh as we always laughed at the little jokes we enjoyed together. Pray, smile, think of me, pray for me. Let my name be ever the household word that it always was. Let it be spoken without effect, without the trace of a shadow on it. Life means all that it ever meant. It is the same as it ever was; there is unbroken continuity. Why should I be out of mind because I am out of sight? I am waiting for you, for an interval, somewhere very near, just round the corner; all is well."

I've grown to understand that we all grieve in our own time, and in our own personal way, while the good Lord provides us with his grace and strength.

Although my tears flowed throughout the reading, I was at least able to read through it. I had been thinking of my son, Brendan since his birthday, which was closely followed by Thanksgiving and Christmas. This continued to be a difficult time of year for me and I needed to fill this yearning for his presence in some way. It is interesting to me that this prayer card happened to be there on my bedside table at a moment when I was somewhat ready to reflect upon what I was about to read. However, the healing process continued to be emotionally difficult.

I fell asleep at about 7:30 P.M. and slept until 11:28 P.M.

As this story unfolds, this hour will prove to be very significant, as it was the time I had awoken and heard my husband quietly enter the bedroom. I continued to lay there, closed my eyes again and began to search my mind for a replay of what I had just dreamed, which was about Brendan and his dad. It was so very real and profound and I wanted to go back to it so I could see my son, Brendan again. However, that didn't happen, but I did fall asleep until the phone rang at the ungodly hour of two in the morning! I got up and went to work and never thought again of my dream.

A couple days later, while riding home in our car, after attending a family memorial service, I began to tell my husband about my dream.

"In my dream, I walked into our kitchen and as I came around the corner of the room, I clearly heard Brendan's voice, as he was talking with you. As I got closer, I saw you both talking and laughing together and I thought to myself, how can this be?! I clearly remember in my dream that Brendan was wearing his blue plaid cotton shirt and I can still see his smiling face as he was helping you put the dishes away. I looked at Brendan, completely astonished, and said to him, *Oh my gosh! It's really you! I thought it was your voice!*

Then Brendan said, 'It's really me!'

I said to him, completely puzzled, *I thought you were gone…I can't believe you are here!*

He just smiled at me as if to say, 'It *is* me and I *am* right here, and you *can* believe it.' Then he gave me a most incredible hug, like he had been away and had come home for a visit. It was certainly weird, but wonderful, dramatic, amazing, and powerful, that I was actually with him!!"

My husband was in awe as he listened intently to the specifics of my dream and then he said to me,

"I wondered when you were going to tell me *something* about that night!" Then he began to tell me about his remarkable experience that occurred *while I was sleeping.*

"It was about 10:30 in the evening and I was relaxing in my chair, after I had finished with the dishes." (My husband's chair is in the corner of our living room, just a few feet from the area in the kitchen where, in my dream, I saw him talking with Brendan and putting the dishes away). My husband continued to say, "As I was sitting in my chair, I saw what looked like bright lights shining through the oval window of the front door. Then I got up to look and seconds later, I saw what looked like a movement of air or a shadow quickly walking by the front door heading towards the bedroom where you were sleeping. I could *feel* Brendan's presence and I could *see* this "breaking of air or movement of air," or shadow, quickly walking by, as if one would see a person quickly walking by."

Puzzled by what he had seen, my husband remained sitting in his chair, as he attempted to make some sort of sense out of something that made absolutely no sense at all! He was feeling very perplexed and began to question whether he imagined the whole thing or if there was something wrong with his eyesight, yet in his heart, he knew it was all true, and he cherished all that he had seen. Also, it was uncanny that my dream of Brendan was occurring during the same hour my husband was witnessing this "movement of air" towards the bedroom! I said to my husband,

"It just so happens that your birthday was the 9th of November. Maybe Brendan was visiting you to wish you a happy birthday. Remember, he never needed to be reminded of special dates."

That little comment put a smile on my husband's face. Although he doesn't always express how he feels, I know this whole experience meant a lot to him, for a dad's heart yearns for his son, too.

Then, my husband, recalled an incident that occurred one morning about two months after his mom died. On that particular morning, he had walked into her living room to get something he needed from her sewing room. As he walked out of her apartment, I heard him say, "Hi, Gracie," as he used to call her and he told me his mom was sitting on her couch where she often sat and watched television. Seconds later, I dashed into her apartment, but she was gone. That is exactly where I had last seen her on the night before she died; she and my son, Brendan, were watching the news together.

It never ceases to amaze me how moments such as these

79

remain so incredibly special. She was a wonderful lady. I still ask for her help and guidance when I'm sewing and especially if I'm having trouble with the sewing machine!

Her death was very sudden and unexpected, nine years earlier, on October 1, 1997, so this was a beautiful and fulfilling experience for my husband, who missed her so very much. She was always a very important part of our lives and her death left a great void, both for us and our children who loved her dearly. Re-telling this experience about his mother helped him to realize that although what he had seen this morning was not an everyday occurrence, it definitely validated that the image he saw was true.

Having a willingness to trust in the supernatural is a blessing when an event such as this cannot be explained in a way our minds can grasp or understand. It was gratifying and comforting to discuss with each other what we both had experienced, knowing and believing Brendan is always with us, even though we realize it is sometimes beyond the realm of our human understanding. One day, in eternity, all the pieces of the puzzle will fit neatly and perfectly together and we will finally understand.

Brendan was very close to his grandmother, Grace, and missed her tremendously after she was gone, but we know today, they are very happily together, enjoying the fruits of their labors.

Chapter 19 - I Am With You Always

On the morning of January 17, 2008, my husband, Bob, heard someone calling his name, but when he looked, no one was there. I listened intently as he told me his story....

"As I was lying in bed trying to fall asleep, I clearly heard the bedroom door open. I reached my hand over to your side of the bed, thinking perhaps it was you leaving the room, but I saw you were sound asleep. Then I heard a quiet voice. The voice was whispering.... '*Dad....Dad*'....which seemed to be coming from the doorway. I turned over in bed to see who was calling me, but the bedroom door was closed and I didn't see anyone there, which was all a bit puzzling. I got out of bed and walked into the living room assuming I would see who had come in, but there was nobody present anywhere in the house. I asked Rob (our son) if he had stopped by our house earlier that morning, as he sometimes does on his way to work, but he had not."

It remained a mystery. As my husband sat in our sun room sipping his cup of coffee, he knew in his heart it had to have been our son, Brendan. He felt his closeness and his love as he thought to himself, "It's not my birthday and it's not a special occasion; I guess he just felt like coming by to say hello." As he spoke, a smile came upon his face and he said to me, "It's been a while, hasn't it?"

Later, I glanced through my journal to see what I had written on the previous days and I read about how I was especially missing Brendan on the 15th of January when I had a deep yearning for his presence. To me, it seemed he had drifted far, far away and I was experiencing a deep longing to feel his presence again. It had been quite some time since I had felt that strong, spiritual connection to him, which always gave me a feeling of hopefulness, peace, and tranquility. On that day I had sat in prayer and meditation in front of the Blessed Sacrament. This is where I go when my heart is congested and I need to simply let the tears flow. I can always talk to Jesus and Mary because I know without a doubt, they will understand my sadness and the uneasiness of my heart. I can truly express everything to them without limitation and I know they will never tire of listening to me. After a while, my heart feels lighter and once again I am rejuvenated.

My husband and I discussed what I had written and we talked about it for a while. It was something we both needed to do that morning. It seemed like Brendan was in the room with us as we reminisced about our treasured memories. In our hearts, we believed he wanted us to know…*"Yes, it was me who entered the room early this morning."* We could almost hear him say… *"I am with you always. Thank you for believing."* We both knew Brendan was the "mysterious person" who had whispered to my husband and had entered our room.

My conclusion is that Brendan knew I was sound asleep, so I wouldn't hear him…..and he was right! He knew his dad would tell me all about what happened, which he did! He knew I would know it was him….which I did! That was his way of confirming his presence to us both.

He also knew his dad was missing him just as much as I had been and wanted to say in his own, very special way, without intruding,

"I'm right here, Dad!! I love you! Please tell Mom I am with you both… always." Thank you, Brendan, so much! We love you too!

I would like to conclude with the following soothing words of encouragement, which my husband and I often reflect upon, whenever our hearts need a gentle uplift:

Grief….

Like the ocean, comes in waves,
Only to recede and come, yet again,
But with it comes healing.
Memories wash ashore,
And are bathed by the golden sun.
Grab hold of these memories,
And let them fill the emptiness.

Author Unknown.

Chapter 20 - The Unlikely Did Happen

On the evening of April 10, 2008, my husband realized an important document was missing from its folder. We had looked in all the possible places, including the folder itself, but to no avail; our diligent search was unsuccessful!

It was April 11, 2008 and I was enjoying the day with two of my precious grandsons, Nicholas, age five and Luke, just six months old. I am so very grateful they live nearby and I thank the Lord I have this opportunity to be with them since their company surely fills my heart with gladness!

At about noontime, Luke was snuggled in his crib, and sound asleep. Knowing his baby brother would nap for a while, Nicholas asked with hopeful anticipation, "Gramma, do you want to play cars with me?"

"Sure!" I answered, as I was always happy to spend one-on-one quality time with him. Earlier that morning he had methodically set up the tracks and had the matchbox cars all lined up and ready for us to pick our favorite ones for the race! I will always cherish these very special moments as I look back over the years and "remember when." I believe children have a wonderful way of demonstrating how to live in the present moment, something I have yet to learn!

After a little while, our game was interrupted when I noticed a reflection of light shining on the wall beside us where we were sitting on the playroom floor. I knew it wasn't sunlight since it was drizzling rain outside. After a few seconds, I saw this same flickering ball of light, about a foot off the floor at eye level, quickly pass by and enter the kitchen through the doorway of the playroom.

Interestingly, I have a photo of Brendan standing in that exact spot, on July 18, 2003, when we first began the construction of our house. Brendan was trying to tune into a radio station, but nothing would come in except Spanish music. I remember we were both feeling very silly and couldn't stop laughing; Even though it had been nearly five years prior, this priceless moment was in the forefront of my memory, and I never thought another thing about it until now. I felt Brendan's warm and loving presence and I felt completely at peace. I took a deep breath and smiled as I said to myself, "I love you," wanting to thank him for always being close by.

At that point, Nicholas glanced over his shoulder, indicating that he, too, had seen something. Then he quickly stood up, closed the door, and remarked to me reassuringly, "There's no one in here, Gramma, just you and me!" Then he sat back down and resumed playing with his cars. "Let's play, Gramma," he said, as though nothing unusual had happened. I sat down on the floor with him and we continued playing with the cars. Nothing more was said. A little while later, Luke awoke from his nap and it was time for us to leave and meet Vincent, their big brother, at the school bus, so off we went.

Evening came, and as I returned home and walked into the house, my husband smiled and asked very inquisitively,

"Where did you find that document?" I looked at him, quite baffled, since I had no idea it had reappeared!

Then we sat down and told one another about the day's events as best we could. I described what happened while Nicholas and I were in the playroom, including the reaction and comment that Nicholas had made, which validated I wasn't the only one who witnessed this flickering light.

Next my husband told me he prayed to Saint Anthony while driving home, asking him to help us find this important paper. The whereabouts of this document had consumed him all day long. Explaining further, he shared that he arrived home and walked to the counter to check the mail. Pleasantly surprised, he realized that this was the missing document, neatly placed on top of the other mail! Then, together we said a quiet little prayer to Saint Anthony, to thank him.

We will admit there is no logical explanation for any of this, but we do know that Brendan and perhaps my dad, probably had something to do with it, as they had a little chat with the faithful patron saint of lost articles, Saint Anthony! Most importantly, we owe all this strange phenomena to the honor and glory of our mighty God and wonder worker! Some things, we just don't question!

84

Chapter 21 - Hug From Heaven

It was the end of a very busy day and as I was getting ready to settle for the night, I was desperately missing my son, Brendan, and his magnificent hugs. I sat on the edge of my bed, and while stretching my arms out to him as far as I could reach, I cried out to him, "I just miss you so much, Brendan!" I was in a terrible state and couldn't stop crying. How I longed for him! My heart was aching and I felt a deep yearning for his warm, physical embrace but couldn't do anything about it! Eventually, feeling emotionally exhausted, I lay down and fell asleep.

At about three o'clock in the morning, I awoke to the sounds from my television set and a program I always enjoy watching on Eternal Word Television Network. About fifteen or twenty minutes later, feeling a bit restless, I got out of bed and ambled into the other room. Eventually I lay down again and said a few prayers to help me fall asleep, as I so often do if I awake during the night.

What seemed to be just a couple minutes later, as I was lying there with my eyes still closed, I felt a gentle rolling sensation across my stomach. I thought perhaps it was a toss pillow or a stuffed animal that happened to be next to me in the bed, but as I reached for whatever had apparently fallen, I realized nothing was there. I distinctly remember hesitating for a few seconds, and as I attempted to sit up, I was held back by "something." I couldn't understand why I couldn't sit forward and I began to feel a bit perplexed because it didn't make any sense to me. Then a second time, I tried to sit forward, but I couldn't, due to this same light pressure.

Then suddenly and very clearly, the answer shot through my mind!! It was Brendan!! I knew it was him! And I said to him, almost gasping with excitement, "Oh my gosh…It's you, Brendan!!" Then in a flash… he was gone. I sat up in bed, feeling bewildered yet awestruck of what had just happened in a period of about one or two minutes. I wanted to reach out and touch him but it was too late. Still, I was convinced of the only possible explanation! I had poured out my heart to him of my need for his hug and I firmly believe he heard me, despite the fact that I will never understand the logistics of it. I know it all sounds peculiar and questionable but I know what I felt at that crucial moment. I own it; it's mine, and no one can take it away from me!

As I lay back down onto the bed, I began to reflect upon this brief interlude I had experienced with Brendan, thinking it through in slow motion. I wanted to take it all in and not miss anything or forget any fraction of it. Then I tucked it all into my treasured bank of memories!

Several days went by and I eventually shared what happened with my daughter, Lisa. Until that time, I hadn't told anyone else about it. I wanted to keep it to myself in that very private and personal place deep within my heart. After I explained everything that happened, she suggested that perhaps Brendan could have been lying there next to me with his arm outstretched across my stomach, which would account for the gentle pressure I had felt, which seemingly prevented me from being able to sit up. Then we concluded we will never truly understand any of it until one day when we are together again.

The date this all occurred, which was April 28, 2008, is very significant, being the seventh wedding anniversary of my daughter, Lisa, and her husband, Leigh. As I write this portion of my book, it occurs to me that perhaps Brendan "chose" this date because he wanted me to reflect upon their wedding day, remembering all the dancing, joy, laughter, happiness and hugs throughout their wedding celebration, which he too, was a great part of, on that beautiful wedding day.

On Easter Sunday afternoon, April 24, 2011, just four days before their tenth wedding anniversary, my son-in-law, Leigh, shared a beautiful story with me regarding Brendan, and his meaningful and unforgettable hugs.

"I remember it so well. I can still feel him like he's right here. On the night Lisa and I got home from our honeymoon, Brendan ran up to us and said to me, 'Now I can **really** call you brother,' and he gave me a huge hug! He wouldn't let go!" Then with tears in his eyes, Leigh said to me, "It was at that exact moment I really felt like part of the family. It meant so much to me. I have shared this special memory with Lisa many, many times before Brendan passed away."

Then Leigh and I reminisced about how thoughtful and genuine Brendan was and how we greatly miss his physical presence. Still thinking of him, we gave each other a big hug. We miss him so very much and we always will, but we thank God every day for all our treasured memories.

Chapter 22 - The Unseen Presence

Saturday, July18, 2009, began with an unexpected phone call from the nurse at 5:30 in the morning, providing an option for me to be on call. This meant she would notify me if our maternity unit became busy. Since it was my turn to take advantage of this offer, I gladly accepted. This was the beginning of the Lord's perfect plan and purpose for my day, as this story will describe.

It was to be a special day set aside in our dad's honor. His fifth anniversary Mass was to be celebrated at St. Rose of Lima Church at five o'clock in the evening. Following Mass, we planned to get together for a leisurely dinner. Whenever our family gets together, we have a great time sharing memories as we reminisce about all the fun we had as kids growing up in a family of thirteen!

My dad was on my mind a lot during the course of the day. Early in the morning, I turned on the television set and a violinist was playing beautiful music to the song, "Holy God We Praise

Thy Name." This melody always reminds me of going to church services, especially benediction, at a little chapel with my father. I can actually visualize him with a few of the other kids like it was yesterday. As I listened to the music and felt his closeness, I said repeatedly, "I love you, Dad, so very much." Truly, this was *his special day.*

It had been five years since we were all together with him in the hospital room, which was an evening I will never forget. The following morning on July 15, 2004, my dad passed away, just ten months after my son, Brendan. I picture them together very happy in the joys of heaven, usually telling each other a joke or two!

At 1:45 P.M. in the afternoon, as I was cleaning the shower in my bathroom, I heard the fan come on. Rather puzzled, I turned around and looked, but no one was there. Then, somehow I *knew* it was my dad! I thought perhaps he was telling me the fan should be on, so I wouldn't breathe in the strong fumes of the cleaner! Although I could barely speak, and I was filled with excitement, I ran out to the kitchen to tell my husband the fan came on, all by itself! He thought perhaps that he should check to see if there was a loose connection. I reassured him not to worry and said to him,

"It's just my dad! I know it! I think he's just letting us know he is glad the family is getting together for Mass and dinner tonight!"

A couple minutes later, when I returned to the bathroom where I was cleaning the shower, the fan was still on. I glanced at my wrist watch; it was 1:52 P.M. Then I said to my dad, "I know it's you! I don't want Bob to go up on the roof for no reason, to check on something that doesn't need fixing! If it's you, could you turn the fan off? I promise I won't be scared," and I stood there, not expecting anything to happen. However, after about ten seconds, **the fan went off!!** Although I was totally unprepared, I knew my dad was answering me and I just stood there in awe! How could that possibly be! I quickly ran out to the kitchen and told my husband what had just happened! Nothing like this had ever happened before and I was dumbfounded by it all. Then I said to my husband,

"I guess Dad doesn't want you climbing onto the roof-top to try to fix something that isn't broken…He wants you to know there's nothing wrong with the fan!" At that point, my husband said,

"Your dad is welcome here anytime!" He loved my dad so much and misses those days when he stopped by for a visit, or came by to help him when we were building our house. Always with a sense of humor, it was the bright spot of the day when my father was around.

After this, I began to feel really emotional! With tears in my eyes, I said, "Dad, if you and Brendan are together exceedingly happy in the heights of heaven, will you turn the fan on again?" However, a second later, my heart knew I was taking advantage of the situation and was expecting too much. I apologetically said to my dad,

"I'm sorry; I absolutely **know** you are together in the heights of heaven. My faith tells me so and I don't need any proof. Thank you, Dad, for everything! I love you so much! Please give Brendan a big hug for me and tell him I love him so very much."

I knew the Lord had to have allowed this all to happen since he alone is in charge of everything and this obviously was purely divine. It's a good thing Bob was home at the time or I might have thought I had imagined the whole thing, but I'm sure God arranged all that too! At that point, I decided to let it all go, feeling very blessed for what had just occurred, while still trying to absorb it all.

Next I decided to call my daughter, Lisa, because I needed to tell someone!! She too, loved her grandfather and missed him very much. She felt a special connection to him since she was driving his car, which he had sold to her just a couple weeks before he passed away. I remember the evening when he signed over the title; my dad was in the hospital and knew he wouldn't be driving anymore. However, never losing his sense of humor, he jokingly added in a sophisticated tone of voice, "champagne beige….lovely color!!" He was differentiating it from just plain beige! He was so happy that his granddaughter was the proud new owner of his car and she was deeply honored as well!

When I told her about the fan, she didn't know what to

say except that it was a truly amazing story, yet very bizarre. She also suggested I not share this with the waitress over dinner that evening! She knew I probably would be talking about it with all the rest of my family, during dinner.

I hung up the phone from my daughter and excitedly phoned my mom as I was still "bouncing off walls," and needed to continue talking about what had just happened! I knew it would be too noisy later on at the restaurant and not an appropriate time to fill her in with all the details.

As I dialed her telephone number from my bedroom phone, I glanced at the time on my watch. It was 2:00 P.M. As I was telling my mom the story, I sensed my dad was very glad I had decided to call her and I knew he wanted to say, "Thanks for sharing everything with mom!" Then...much to my total amazement, **the fan came on!** It was now 2:10 P.M. I blurted out to my mother that the fan came on!! My heart leaped in my chest because this was a confirmation for me that he and Brendan were definitely together, happily rejoicing in the kingdom of heaven! I could barely speak, completely awestruck that the fan came on for the second time by itself!! I knew my dad was answering my question I had asked him earlier; "Yes...Brendan and I *are* together, exceedingly happy, in the heights of heaven!"

As I was explaining all this to my mother and we were about to end our conversation, **the fan turned off!!** It was now 2:17 P.M! Since then, the fan has never turned on or turned off by itself again!!

I often hear Brendan encouraging me with words of comfort as he gently reminds me, "The Lord is always listening and hears all your prayers." I also hear him saying, "Fix your eyes on Jesus, or "Where's your faith, Mom?"

Most importantly, I believe that our dad wanted to tell us how happy he was that many of his children would be at Mass for his very special memorial. My dad oftentimes wanted to know which Mass we attended and it was meaningful that we practiced on a weekly basis. Today, watching over us from above, he continues to pray for all of us here on earth and watches over us from his eternal home in heaven, at the dawning of each new day!

A few days later, my mother reminded me about the fan

incident that occurred a day or two after my dad passed away. She clearly remembered turning the fan off and when she went back into the bedroom, it was on again. I did recall this incident and this was, in fact, the reason I knew it was my dad, who again was playing games with the fan in our shower on July 18, 2009! I'm sure he was having a great time, I might add! He probably had Brendan going right along with him!

Our loved ones are always very near as they continue to communicate their love and blessings to us according to God's plan. We are all part of the Communion of Saints and are privileged to pray to them, for them and with them.

Today, on May 25, 2010 I planned to write about this particular story, and very interestingly after morning Mass, I heard the beautiful sounds of the church bells echoing this tune: "Holy God We Praise Thy Name." I felt my precious dad's nearness, warmth and embracing love and I knew.... "He's right here!" I dedicate this song to him as I hear the melody playing in my head.....

Holy God we praise thy name
Lord of all, we bow before thee!
All on earth, thy scepter claim,
All in heaven above adore thee.
Infinite thy vast domain,
Everlasting is thy reign,
Hark! The loud celestial hymn
Angel choirs above are raising,
Cherubim and seraphim,
In unceasing chorus praising;
Fill the heavens with sweet accord;
Holy, holy, holy Lord.

I love you, Dad...Thank you for everything you did and still do for all of us.

Chapter 23 - We Believe

Brendan was deeply missed by all the family, most especially by his grandparents, Kathleen and Leo McLaughlin, who always had a very special relationship with him. He would often stop by their house and offer to mow the lawn, shovel the snow, or just stop by for a surprise visit.

Brendan's Grampa was well known for his "Leo jokes" and when they got together, joy filled the room with the sound of laughter. Christmas, birthdays, Mother's Day, and Father's Day, were all important and special to him and he would always bring a unique gift for the occasion. One year, Brendan bought his grandfather a rain gauge for his birthday, which he absolutely loved! Every time it rained, like a little kid with a new toy, my dad would go outside to measure the inches of rainfall! Then he would say, "Oh well, we really needed the rain," even if it had been raining for days!

His grandmother, too, has several of his special gifts in her home, including a "footprints in the sand" prayer plaque on a small stand, which remains a memorable keepsake. My mom and I were admiring it on Mother's Day, 2010, thinking about both Brendan and my dad, who we sorely miss, but believe are together having their own celebration. In a reminiscent tone of voice, my mom said to me with a smile on her face,

"I remember when Brendan gave it to me, right on time for Mother's Day, but took it back to have it engraved for me." Together, my mom and I read, *Happy Mother's Day... 1999*
Love, Brendan.

These words were beautifully engraved on a small, gold plate. I could hear his gentle voice and feel his loving presence on this special day, like he was right there beside us, glad we were enjoying our day. "Happy Mother's Day," I heard him say and with tears in my eyes, I smiled while remembering the years past. He always surprised us with the perfect Mother's Day gifts. How we missed him, especially on this day.

The week following Brendan's passing in September of 2003, my mother received little messages that she knew were clearly from him. These messages were received not in the same way we hear the spoken word, but as words "running through her mind."

It was just a day or two after the funeral of her grandson, as she knelt in quiet meditation before the Blessed Sacrament at St. Peter's Church in Plymouth, Massachusetts. In the quiet stillness, she heard Brendan say very clearly, "Now I understand," but was puzzled by what he meant by this. She said it was as though he was right there beside her, as she was praying and thinking about him. We both know he *was* there and these were words of peace and comfort for my mom.

She and Brendan often had intimate conversations together, especially when he had questions about certain situations that troubled him. Their conversations set him at ease and gave him peace of mind. Since my mom was praying in front of the Blessed Sacrament when she heard the words, "Now I understand," I thought it was very fitting to include this quote by Pope John Paul 11:

"In the presence of this mystery of the Eucharist, human reason experiences its limitations. The heart, however, responds and bows low in adoration and in love."….from Ecclesia de Eucharistia.

After my mother quoted the words she heard from Brendan, "Now I understand," I later recalled a passage from the Holy Bible, which she read on the 16th of September, at Brendan's eleven o'clock funeral Mass. It reads as follows:

"But the just man, though he dies young, will be at rest. Being made perfect in a short time, he fulfilled long years; his soul pleased the Lord, therefore he hastened to bring him out of the midst of iniquities. Yet the people saw this and did not understand, or take such things to heart, that God's grace and mercy are with his elect, and that he watches over his holy ones."
(Wisdom 4:7, 13-15).

Very often, I listened to Mother Angelica on television and on one particular episode, my ears perked up to a conversation regarding God's permitting will. I had so many questions tugging at my heart, such as, "Why did this have to happen to Brendan?" and "Why did God allow this accident to take his life?"

94

I listened to her explain that the Lord's timing is perfect and that he calls us home when we are in our most perfect state. Her comforting words helped set my heart at ease, especially since I knew Brendan had a personal relationship with Jesus, which had carried over to his caring relationships with everyone he met. Brendan had a host of friends and everyone who knew him also loved him. I was deeply honored at his wake when many crowds of family and friends arrived to offer their condolences and say their last goodbyes.

On another occasion, my mom was swimming in her pool and she looked up into the sunny blue sky as she was thinking about her grandson, Brendan. She clearly heard him say to her,

"Nana, I'm not up there in the sky; I'm right here next to you." Then, on another occasion about a week later, she heard him say,

"Nana, you have no idea how much God loves you!"

Another time she heard him say,

"Nana, it's so beautiful here!"

My mom describes these messages as "words that run through her mind with perfect clarity," and she knows, without a doubt, that it is Brendan who is speaking to her.

I believe my mother has a supernatural gift to receive these messages through Divine Intervention, giving me the hope and courage to continue God's work. She is a very spiritual woman who loves God and He blessed her with the inspiration of the Holy Spirit, to relay to me what is necessary for my spiritual growth. We both know Brendan is at a place of eternal joy and beauty beyond our human understanding. It seems whenever I am at the brink of despair and crying out to the Lord for help, he always rescues me in a phenomenal way with the help of others or from reading Scripture verses from the Bible.

"God's love does not impose burdens upon us that we cannot carry, nor make demands of us that we cannot fulfill. For whatever He asks of us, He provides the help that is needed," are very encouraging words spoken by Pope John Paul 11.

"God is faithful and will not let you be tried beyond your strength; but with the trials He will also provide a way out, so that you may be able to bear it" (1 Corinthians 10: 13).

It was Thanksgiving Day of the year 2003, just two and one half months after the tragic death of my son, Brendan. My shattered heart ached with unbearable pain and I realized I had no control because I couldn't do anything to change what had happened. It seemed that time had stood still; I couldn't get past a day ago, let alone a week or a month. Now two and one half months had passed, but it was all a blur. I felt like I was encapsulated in a cloud of despair and I couldn't get out! I was living a nightmare on the outside looking in. I truly identified with Mary, the mother of Jesus, Our Lady of Sorrows, when I read how Simeon foretold to her that "a sword would pierce her heart."

On November 26, 2003, Thanksgiving Day, I was sitting outside on the porch at my daughter and son-in-law's home, thinking about Brendan. (He was born the night before Thanksgiving Day in the year 1975). I was grief-stricken and overcome with deep sadness, but for some reason I got a very strong inspiration to make a phone call to my parents. They too, were completely devastated over Brendan's loss. I believe the Lord knew that I desperately needed some relief from this weight of grief and I dialed their number. My mom answered the phone, almost like she was expecting the call and she said to me,

"I'm so glad you called. I've been wanting to tell you something but I didn't want you to think I'm going senile or anything like that! After all, I am eighty-two years old!"

"Tell me what?" I asked.

Then my mom explained she had been hearing Brendan say repeatedly, with a nagging persistence and a pleading tone…. "Tell my mother I love her."

I asked my mom how long she had been hearing him say this and she said….

"Oh, for about a week now."

I was filled with emotion and I just wanted her to keep repeating to me what she had heard him say. I could almost feel the relief Brendan must have felt once his message finally got to me.

After I hung up the phone, I quietly sat on the porch for quite some time, trying to absorb our conversation, while feeling such a phenomenally, comforting "embrace" from Brendan. It's so difficult to find the words to describe the incredible comfort I felt from him and how I knew he was definitely there with me at that moment. I remember thanking God for helping me receive that incredibly important message, I knew Brendan had been trying to send to me.

Then I tearfully and painfully recalled when I stood by his lifeless body laid upon a stretcher in the emergency room, on the night of the accident, as I said to him, "I love you, I love you, I love you…Oh my God, I love you so much!!"… I couldn't say it enough; the words kept rolling off my tongue. I believe this message relayed to me today, on his birthday, was Brendan's way of telling me he heard me and wanted me to know this, and wanted to say it back to me.

"The Lord is near to the brokenhearted, and saves the crushed in spirit" (Psalm 34:18).

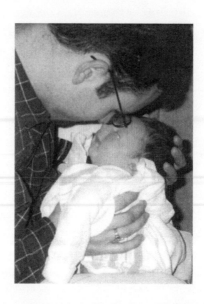

Chapter 24 - Pure Unconditional Love

I vividly remember the birth of my grandson, Nicholas, on March 28, 2003, at 9:36 in the morning. Seconds after his birth, I kissed his precious little face, my heart bursting with love for him, as I said, "Oh how I love you so much…It's so wonderful to finally get to meet you…I'm your Gramma!"

Indeed, I am so very blessed to have had the privilege of witnessing the births of all four of my grandsons!

Later in the evening of this joyous day, amongst a roomful of excited visitors, was baby Nicholas' Uncle Brendan. Soon to follow, was a moment in time I will never cease to forget. As his Uncle Brendan held him snuggly and lovingly with Nicholas' tiny head cupped in his hand, their faces touching nose to nose, and their eyes gently closed, I quickly ran to get my camera, as I called out to him, *"Hold that pose!"*

Seconds later, I returned; it was at that moment I knew I had to capture this beautiful and lasting image of the two of them together. Surely, timing was everything! That one and only photograph of Nicholas, at about nine hours old with his Uncle Brendan, would be a priceless, treasured keepsake. Every time I gaze upon this memorable pose, I see a memory of pure love, a picture of sheer contentment reflecting an inner peace between them, enveloped in a quiet stillness that evening.

Five and a half months later, the reason was clear to me regarding why I felt it was so important to take that very special photo, when on September 11, 2003, Nicholas' Uncle Brendan was no longer with us. I will be forever grateful that I was inspired to take advantage of a once in a lifetime opportunity. There are no coincidences with God.

Over the next several months, my husband and I stayed with my daughter and her family. Each morning as I came downstairs, I was greeted by my precious grandson, Nicholas, who would crawl over to me as I got to the bottom of the staircase. As I picked him up and lovingly held him in my arms, I felt a deep contentment and a peace that was beyond words. It was surely an enormous gift of grace that enabled me to go on, one day at a time. Because I believe the trusting hearts and minds of babies and young children are closely united with Jesus and his angels in heaven, I felt a consolation and a closeness to Brendan as I held onto my baby grandson, Nicholas.

One morning, I was standing in the kitchen of my daughter's home, staring out the window and feeling a million miles away. While holding Nicholas in my arms, I heard his little cooing sounds as he was looking over my shoulder and smiling at "someone or something," although Nicholas and I were the only ones in the room. Perhaps Brendan knew I was desperately missing him and he was there at that difficult moment to somehow bring me some solace and relief. Looking at Nicholas' precious little face, I tearfully asked him,

"Do you see Uncle Brendan?"

In my heart, I *knew* that he could. And somehow, I believed that he understood my sadness, and I felt an incredible comfort and sense of peacefulness while holding him in my arms. The unconditional love of a baby, blended with this same unconditional love a grandparent has for her grandbaby was undeniable! I could confide in my precious six month old grandson, Nicholas, and feel his love and support! It was all that I needed and my heart was infused with an immeasurable dose of consolation. I didn't need to justify, explain or defend myself to anyone because I knew what I felt. I sat down with Nicholas in my arms and had a "private conversation" with Brendan and told him over and over again how much I loved him and missed him, while asking him to "please stay close by me." For a long time, I felt his very strong and loving presence as I sat in the rocking chair, holding Nicholas in my arms, and feeling absolute peace. I believe the Lord was helping me through this very difficult and overwhelming crisis of my life, with the help of a precious baby to focus my attention upon and count my blessings every day. God promises he will not give us more than we can handle and he offers us sufficient grace to process our pain. He is faithful to all his promises.

At the end of my shift on a Thursday afternoon in October of 2004, my faithful co-workers presented me with a hologram of my son, Brendan, which had his image engraved on a gold pendant. They had copied this photo from his memorial prayer card. As I opened this totally unexpected gift and saw Brendan's face smiling back at me, I was filled with emotion and my eyes overflowed with tears. I said to them,

"You guys could have given me a million dollars and it wouldn't have meant anything to me compared to this!"

I was so very grateful but couldn't find the exact words to express just how much! After admiring the pendant repeatedly, amazed at this perfectly sketched image of my son and feeling like he was right there smiling back at me, I placed it around my neck. Not a single day goes by that I don't think of him and I tell him every day I love him with all my heart.

At nineteen months old, Nicholas would often clasp the pendant between his tiny fingers, kiss the image of my son, and very lovingly, place the pendant to my lips so I would do the same. I had never consciously told him it was his Uncle Brendan, but he just somehow seemed to know. It was like his heart understood and felt in a very tender, gentle, childlike way what I was experiencing. We had developed a very special bond of unconditional love and trust; what an incredible gift I had received with the birth of this beautiful child of God!

Today, seven years later, my youngest grandson, Luke,

who is a very bright and spunky two year old, frequently takes a hold of the pendant I am wearing, kisses it, then says to me, "Who's this, Uncle Brendan??" Then he smiles at me and places the pendant on my lips to do the same!! He is quite the amazing two year old!

It is very apparent to me that babies and young children are very close to Jesus and things of a spiritual nature. My own personal experiences relating to my grandchildren about which I have written in this book, speaks volumes to this truth.

Recently, I was told this story, which I thought was absolutely amazing and I would like to share it with you.

A little five year old girl asked her mom if she could spend a few minutes alone with her baby sister, newly home from the hospital. Her mom gave her permission, but was curious as to why she made this request. As she listened quietly at the doorway of the bedroom, she heard her daughter ask her baby sister…

"Can you please tell me what Jesus looks like? I can't remember."

A few minutes later, as the little girl left the room, she was smiling and she said to her mom, "Thanks Mom. I feel better now," and off she went, without giving her mom a chance to respond. As written above, this story confirmed my beliefs that babies and young children do have an undefined yet very special relationship with Jesus.

Another true story I would like to share is about a young child who was autistic. His parents wanted to bring him to church on Sunday mornings, but were embarrassed because of his misbehavior. However, one morning, they decided to stay until after the Consecration of the Mass. They noticed the young boy immediately became very quiet during this part of the Mass. His attention was fixed on the Elevation of the Host and the Chalice. Seeing this, his parents believed their son was seeing angels, although not visible to them, during the Consecration.

I will continue to believe that during the Consecration of the Mass, heaven opens up to the earth and hosts of angels are present on the altar. As Saint Francis de Sales tells us, "Make yourselves familiar with the angels, and behold them frequently in spirit; for without being seen, they are present with you."

Chapter 25 - Yet to be Revealed

It was a clear night on September 11th of 2003, as my son, Brendan drove along, listening to one of his favorite tunes he had plugged into his CD player. He had spent the evening visiting with his sister, Lisa, and nephews, Vincent and Nicholas and was on his way home to his brother, Rob's house with his nephew, "little Brendan," snuggled in his car seat.

Suddenly, something caused his 1999 Chevy Blazer to stop suddenly and swerve abruptly, leaving several feet of skid marks behind his path. Suddenly, the vehicle rolled over, severely crushing the roof. What obstructed his view that evening at 10:05 P.M? Very sadly, we realize we will never know for sure; we can only make an educated guess and remain in a state of curiosity as to what happened.

My grandson, little Brendan said he saw a "polar bear" run across the street! Others have reported this area is the perfect hunting ground for deer and have often seen them darting across the road. Since Brendan's accident, I have seen vehicles, especially during hunting season, pulled over and parked on the grassy slopes in this same location on Interstate 195. After hearing about the possibility of a deer obstructing Brendan's view and causing the accident, my niece, Renée, recalls the most amazing and mysterious happening! She explained,

"I was thinking about Brendan, and looking up into the sky beyond the tree branches, I saw a cloud that looked like a deer looking at me!!" (See back cover)

She couldn't believe what she was seeing, and knew she had to take a photo! Was this Brendan's answer in the sky, trying to tell her that is exactly what happened? Will this remain "just a piece of the puzzle"?

Renee and her husband, Brian, also recall their telephone rang at 11:00 P.M. on the night of September 11.th "No one ever calls us at this hour," they said with great concern. Brian picked up the receiver, but no one answered. The next morning, they knew that it was Brendan wanting to say goodbye.

About a week after we laid our son to rest, we planted grass seed over his sacred burial ground. I can't actually remember, but we must have watered it with our tears as we tried to console each other, still numb with grief. Every day, I went back there to talk to him on my way home from morning Mass at St. Rose of Lima Church, where his funeral had taken place just a week earlier.

Brendan's fiancée and I had very methodically placed little green apples that had fallen from the tree nearby all around where the seed had been planted to carefully outline this area. Somehow, this gave us comfort to know where Brendan's body was laid to rest. I know the Lord must have been holding onto me very, very tightly that day as well as the weeks and months to follow because it is still beyond my comprehension how I made it through!

Today, as I stood by his gravesite praying to, with, and for him, I noticed fresh, new shoots of green grass beginning to sprout. Then, as I looked closer my eyes caught sight of what I considered to be, perhaps another "hint" from Brendan. The area where we planted the seed was decorated in deer tracks!! I immediately grabbed my camera to get a photo of the evidence! As silly as this probably sounds, I remember I was thinking at that moment, "the entire family of deer are telling me how terribly sorry they are for causing the accident!" After all, the Lord does have a sense of humor and he certainly knew I needed some cheering up!

Many times during the next several weeks, as my husband and I drove through the cemetery after dusk, we frequently saw three or four deer running across our path just a few feet in front of us! We wondered if this was just a coincidence or was this a sign from above telling us a deer did, in fact, dart out into the roadway that night.

Approximately six or seven months later, I attended a conference with a friend of mine. On our way home, while driving from Middleboro to Rochester, a huge deer literally flew in front of my windshield! It looked like a brown blur all within one second of time! Just before this happened, my friend Kathy and I were talking about Brendan and how unreal it seemed that he was no longer with us, and how we will never know what caused the accident. Then, all of a sudden, this huge brown animal was directly in front of me and I didn't have time to think. I was simply flabbergasted! All I could say over and over was, "Did you see that!" I was so grateful we were alive and talking to one another trying to figure out how we escaped a serious accident! It all happened so quickly. If my friend wasn't there as my witness, I might have thought I was imagining the whole scene!

After Brendan's horrible accident, I couldn't stop thinking about what happened. Was he scared? What went through his mind? Did he feel pain? I couldn't sleep at night, as I was frequently waking up having nightmares. I wished I could have been with him to take care of him!! I believe Brendan wanted to tell me, "Everything happened so quickly, Mom; I didn't have time to be afraid. Next I knew I was in the loving arms of Jesus and our Blessed Mother, Mary…I was never alone."

Although this incident had been a very frightening experience for me, now I had a better understanding of what probably happened with my son on the night of his accident. It was the Lord's way of helping me to let go of trying to control something I had no control over, and to realize there was nothing I could have done to help my son or to change anything. Perhaps the Lord also used this incident to give me the consolation and reassurance I needed, combined with a message of love from Brendan, since my son knew I would make the connection. Yes...*He's right here*, all the time, close by me, helping me be aware of God's grace and immense love that continues to sustain me with courage and peace, with new hopes and new dreams that can actually come true if I trust and rely upon God. If I take one step toward Him, He takes ten towards me! Brendan says to me often, "Keep your eyes fixed on Jesus," so I try to do that, especially when I'm having flashbacks of traumatic experiences or obsessing about the many unanswered questions that persistently trouble me.

This story wouldn't be complete if I didn't mention a summer night in 2004, when we were greeted by "unexpected guests"! Upon returning home at about midnight, as we entered our driveway, there stood a buck, a doe, and a fawn! It was a perfect picture of "deer caught in the headlights," as they stood and looked at us completely baffled for at least a minute! We, of course, were totally amazed as well, since we had never experienced anything like this before this night! Once they gained their composure, off they ran across our yard into the woods, since we had spoiled all their fun! My husband and I just sat there for several minutes and thought about Brendan.

Just a few days ago, I drove up my driveway, parked my car in the garage, and as I walked around my car and looked across my yard, I saw, again, a buck, a doe, and her fawn, all three of them standing very still, looking back at me! Before this time, I had never seen a family of deer in the mid-afternoon, hanging out in my back yard! Of course I took a photo to show my husband when he came home. Then, he told me about a deer he saw earlier in the week standing at the edge of our lawn and watching a squirrel! We're not sure of the significance of our new-found friends, but when we see them we **always** think of Brendan and feel his love because we know he's right here beside us.

Brendan was a loyal member of the International Brotherhood of Electrical Workers, employed as a telecommunications technician. He was well-loved and appreciated by his fellow workers, and his unexpected loss was met with great sadness. In loving memory of Brendan, with their heartfelt condolences and deepest sympathy, the IBEW members presented us with a Bible, embossed with beautiful, gold lettering, and the "Dove of Peace" insignia on its soft, white cover in a decorative, polished cedar case. I was so touched when I opened it and read on the inside cover of the case, a poem called "The Plan of the Master Weaver." I thought of Brendan, as my heart filled with emotion while I read the following:

My life is but a weaving
    Between the Lord and me,
I may not choose the colors,
    He knows what they should be;
For He can view the pattern
    Upon the upper side.
Sometimes he weaveth sorrow,
    Which seemeth strange to me;
But I will trust His judgment
    And work on faithfully;
Tis He who fills the shuttle,
    And He knows what is best,
So I shall weave in earnest,
    Leaving to Him the rest.
Not 'til the loom is silent
    And the shuttles cease to fly,
Shall God unroll the canvas
    And explain the reason why--
The dark threads are as needed
    In the Weaver's skillful hand,
As the threads of gold and silver
    In the pattern He has planned.

Author Unknown.

One day we will know the answers to life's many puzzles and the pieces will fit perfectly together. That is the day we will be together again eternally happy in heaven, where I know I will see Brendan, my dad, and all those I love and miss. Until then, I will continue to believe with every beat of my heart, "he's right here," just beyond the horizon.

Randomly looking through my Bible today, I came across this very appropriate psalm:

"As the deer longs for streams of water, so my soul longs for you oh God"… taken from psalm 42, verse 1.

There are no coincidences with God. He plans everything! He hears and answers all our prayers. After Brendan was suddenly gone from my life here on this earth, I had a great longing to be with him; to feel his touch and to be near him. I spent hours looking through my Bible, underlining Scripture passages and identifying with what I was reading and it was like Jesus Himself was speaking to me! I felt nourished, and somehow, deeply satisfied and content, (even if it was just for a little while) because I felt a very strong connection to Brendan as my heart told me he was with Jesus. The closer I got to Jesus, the closer I would be to Brendan, and I would be okay for a little while. Our loving God wants us to call on Him, trust in Him, talk to Him as a caring, compassionate and faithful friend because He loves us so much! It took me a long time to really believe this and today I want to share this with the world and shout it from the rooftops!

For anyone who has lost a son or daughter, I urge you to scream out to God and tell him exactly how you feel; He can take it! He understands! He is always right by your side and wants you to turn to him so He can comfort you, but He will never force himself on you. He knows your pain and wants to help, so go to him, and a miracle of healing will happen for you as it did for me.

The shortest verse in the Bible is, "*And Jesus wept.*" as he did at the death of his friend Lazarus… (John chapter 1; verse 35).

May God bless you and may his face shine upon you, as you let these words be absorbed deep within your heart, mind and spirit!

Chapter 26 - My Name is Michael

As I took one tiny step at a time after my son Brendan's untimely death, I was able to reconstruct my life with the assistance of several people who happened across my path. Interestingly, each had the name of "Michael," which was also my son's middle name.

The police officer at the scene of the accident on the evening of September 11, 2003, was named Sergeant *Michael* Downing. He recovered a very special guardian angel prayer card I had given to my son, Brendan, which he had kept in his car. On the night of the accident, it was tossed into the street and the sergeant saw it and saved it for me. He will probably never really know the true depth of my gratitude. It was just a simple card, but oh how meaningful it was for me to hold this special card close to my heart and allow myself to feel my son's warm and loving presence for just a few minutes. Perhaps this sounds insignificant to most, but anyone who has lost a son or daughter, will identify and agree with the importance of special treasures. Of special interest to me is the fact that Saint Michael is the patron saint of policemen.

Earlier that same day, my son, Brendan, had brought his four year old nephew, "Little Brendan" to Friendly's for an ice cream and had won a very special gift for him. It was "Patrick," from his nephew's favorite television show, "Sponge Bob." The kind and thoughtful officer had set "Patrick" aside to save for my grandson and I honestly don't know who was happier about "the return of Patrick," my grandson or me! To this day, Patrick remains a special keepsake; it's the little things that mean so much! The genuine kindness and thoughtfulness of this man will forever be appreciated.

As my son, Brendan, arrived at the emergency room that same night, Father *Michael* Racine was there to attend to his spiritual needs. I will be forever indebted to him for administering the Sacrament of Anointing to my son and praying *with* him during the last moments of his life. I vividly recall thanking him repeatedly for opening the gates of heaven with a golden key after he had administered this great sacramental gift to my well-deserving son, just moments before his joyous and jubilant entry into eternal happiness! I felt a deep abiding peace which saturated my soul with a belief that my beloved son, Brendan, was tenderly received and lovingly embraced in the arms of Almighty God as he heard these welcoming words: "Well-done my good and faithful servant…Enter now into the kingdom of heaven!!"

A few weeks later, as I sat in front of The Blessed Sacrament during Eucharistic Exposition while listening to a song of adoration, these words rang out and echoed into the chambers of my heart: "Faith will tell us Christ is present when our human senses fail." The words of the song were being sung in Latin, "Praestet fides supplementum, sensuum defectui," but I began to meditate upon the English translation for a clearer understanding. This was a confirmation for me; I was convinced Brendan definitely knew *Father Michael was there, anointing him*, as he had reassured me that night on September 11th and I believe my son also knew the Lord was calling him home to be with Him. It was like the floodgates opened for me at that moment and an abundance of grace filled my soul with a consoling peace, helping me to bear the heavy cross I was carrying. Then, I *heard* these words…."My grace is sufficient," and I knew everything was going to be alright, thanks to God and Father *Michael!*

One month after Brendan's funeral, I wandered into a prayer meeting being held at Sacred Heart Church in Middleboro. I sat down in the pew feeling completely broken and desperate. My cousin, Mary, whose daughter had died six years earlier also in a car accident, had suggested I might find some comfort there. Within a few minutes, I was invited to join the prayer group of about seven or eight members, which I eventually did because I was in so much pain. Then I just burst into tears and blurted out, "I'm not here just to pray. My son was killed in a car accident," as I choked on the words, "and I don't know what to do!" With genuine concern, compassion and understanding, they suggested we pray together. At that point in time, I couldn't pray; I was too upset, grief-stricken, confused and completely unable to make sense out of anything! I remember listening to "the Chaplet" from the CD player and the beautiful, soothing music in the background. Then the prayer team brought me to a quiet, peaceful place in the church, the sacristy, and offered to pray with me. While feeling sad, desperate, crushed in my sorrow and needing their help, I accepted their offer. They taught me how to reach out my arms to my son and actually talk to him which brought me tremendous relief! They also explained it was understandable I was angry at God and encouraged me to cry out to Him and tell Him exactly how I felt about His "allowing" this terrible accident to happen, while reminding me the Lord is close to the broken-hearted and he feels our pain.

Although just a beginning, I felt an incredible healing that evening, thanks to these three very special and caring individuals who were placed in my path. I also thank God since I know He helped me listen to my heart's urging to go there that evening and receive this gift of healing!

After praying with me, they invited me to return the following week so they could continue helping me, which again, I graciously accepted. The prayer team members then introduced themselves: Vinnie, Cammie, and *Michael!!!* *It* was his voice and encouragement as well as his name that brought me back the following week, especially when he said, "Come back next week and we'll pray some more for you." There is definitely something very special about the name of Michael!

My mom knows I believe Saint Michael the Archangel was present on the night of the accident, as I alluded to in the beginning entries of this book. His powerful aid has always been invoked by the church in times of emergencies and he is known as the special protector in times of unusual danger. I believe Saint Michael intervened for my grandson, Brendan, and with God's miraculous help, provided him with everything he needed as he was rescued from the wreckage that horrendous night. My mom presented me with a beautiful statue of this special saint, which I have displayed in his honor for all to see. Along with the Saint Michael statue, she had written on a small piece of paper these words:

"Michael is the angel of the transition from time to eternity. The point of his spear is the point where eternity breaks into time, and transforms it, both 'now and at the hour of our death,' as the Hail Mary says."

In October of 2003, my husband and I discussed placing a statue of Saint Brendan, in our son's memory, on the grounds of Saint Rose of Lima Church. After several phone calls and many prayers, I made a phone call to Eden's Garden Supply. I smiled when the voice at the other end of the receiver answered, "Eden Garden Supply, this is *Michael*....What can I do for you?" I certainly knew I had the right place which it proved to be. Interestingly, just across the street was Saint Brendan's Church, which provided Michael with a visual of the statue to give him the description he needed of Saint Brendan!

Eventually, all the arrangements were made for the statue to be shipped from Italy! Nine months later, the beautiful, white marble statue arrived. On July 24, 2004, we had a dedication ceremony with the blessing of the statue, as it stood on the lawn of our family's church, Saint Rose of Lima!! The beautiful white marble statue is mounted on a black granite pedestal and written with black Gaelic-style lettering across the white marble front of the statue is the name.......*ST. BRENDAN*. Written on the front of the black granite pedestal in contrasting white Gaelic-style lettering are the heartwarming words.....

A gift to St. Rose of Lima,

From the McGee and Hodson families,

In honor of Brendan Michael McGee.

Nov 26,1975-Sep 11, 2003.

Brendan's generous and loving fiancée contributed to the purchase of this beautiful statue. Five years later, on June 28, 2008, she married a wonderful man named *Michael!*

On my return to Tobey hospital, five months after my son passed away, I was privileged to be present at the birth of a precious baby boy to a charming couple I had known from a previous delivery. It was always an uplifting experience to witness the birth of a baby regardless of how many births I had attended. Each birth was always a miracle in my eyes! God is so good; being my first day back to work, He wanted it to be an enjoyable day to remember. God has a perfect plan. The dad's name to this beautiful baby boy was also ironically named, *Michael!!*

Brendan had a passion for playing the drums from an

early age of nine years old. Now my grandsons are enjoying his drums at their young ages of three, seven, eleven and twelve. I know Brendan must be smiling down on them all the while! Also, my little nephew, Matthew, at age ten already has an incredible talent for playing the drums! I remember so clearly watching my son beating on his drums, headphones covering his ears, completely engrossed in his music! Whenever I hear the sound of a drum, I immediately think of my son, Brendan. Whenever I watch my grandsons sitting at his drums, I am sure that Brendan remains at their side.

In December of 2003, my husband and I established a music scholarship fund in honor of our son, Brendan Michael. Through a series of "divine interventions," the music fund was established just two months after his tragic, unexpected death. Its purpose is to provide financial support to any interested fourth, fifth, or sixth grade student with an eagerness to play a musical instrument. Also, the music fund continues to award scholarship money toward the full purchase of a musical instrument to a sixth grade band member who will continue his or her music career at the junior high school.

The young, aspiring musicians in the band at the Rochester Memorial School proudly wear their tee shirts, printed with the design of a drum set and with green lettering denoting "The Brendan Michael McGee Music Scholarship Fund." What an amazing tribute to him since he loved playing the drums!

Every year, since we established this wonderful music fund in Brendan's loving memory, we set aside a day on or around the 11th of September, when we celebrate his life and his love. Over the past three years, we have invited a disc jockey from "M.C. Music Productions" to help us celebrate! Interestingly, the "M" stands for none other than... *Michael!!* When making arrangements for this years' celebration, scheduled for September 11, 2011, I spoke to Michael about my book and the significance of this chapter entitled, *My Name is Michael*. Then he told me he has a tattoo of "Michael the Archangel" on his back! That's when I knew for certain he was absolutely the right guy for our special event. When I follow my hearts promptings, everything seems to turn out according to God's perfect plan.

Chapter 27 - Convictions of the Heart

I believe my sister, Angela, perhaps may have a supernatural connection to an "unseen dimension." I say this because she has shared with me certain inexplicable events she has experienced. For example, she explained:

"For about two weeks before Brendan's death, the visor in my car was broken. It kept falling down. After he was gone, I missed him so much and I talked to him all the time, as he was always on my mind. A few days after he died, I said to him:

'Brendan...can you just fix this stupid thing; I'm sick of holding it!'

Realizing this was obviously an unusual request, I took a deep breath, while picturing him beside me. The next day it rained and I didn't use my car. On the following day as I was driving to work, I put the visor down expecting it to fall, but instead, it stayed in place!! At first, I was stunned, and then I thought to myself, 'oh my gosh, it's fixed!' I remembered how I had called out to Brendan to fix it, but now I was totally amazed and I got this indescribable feeling as I realized what had just happened! I looked up into the sky with tears in my eyes because I knew it was Brendan. I said to him...

'Thank you Brendan!! I don't know how you did it but I know it's fixed!' "

Then, she went on to explain:

"Later that same evening, I received an even stronger confirmation when I asked my husband if he had fixed it and he had no idea what I was talking about. Because no other person drives my car, once again, I was convinced that it was Brendan. Today, almost seven years later, I think of Brendan every time I use my visor. Yes….I know, he's right here!!"

On another occasion, Angela was sitting out on her deck thinking about our dad. It was a warm summer evening in August of 2004, only about one month since he had passed on and just eleven months since we lost Brendan.

As she reflected upon her experience, she explained,

"I was feeling particularly sad because I was especially missing Dad that night. Out of the clear blue, I started to hum to the tune of "Red River Valley," which was one of Dad's favorite songs that I often listened to him sing. As I sat there deep in thought and picturing him beside me, I began to feel really chilly, even though it was an especially warm and humid evening. After a few minutes, I said to Dad…*'If you are with me now, show me a sign; just blow my candle out.'* (There was a candle burning on a little table beside her). Then, within a minute of time, it was like someone took their two fingers and snuffed out the flame of the candle, right in front of my eyes! There was no wind and no breeze; I knew Dad was trying to comfort me even if he was there for only a few minutes.

Then I closed my eyes and continued to think about the last time Dad and I danced to the tune of "Red River Valley," which was in August of 1999, while I was in England with my parents, visiting my aunt, uncle and their lifelong friends. I will never forget that fun-filled evening!"

Yet again, as she tells it,

"I was taking a leisurely bath and after about five minutes, I heard my cat jumping around and making a lot of noise. I got out of the tub to see what all the commotion was about. I had left a plain beige sweater, which had belonged to Dad, hanging on the banister outside the bathroom. As I walked out, I couldn't believe my eyes! I looked at the sweater and thought I was seeing things! What had been a plain beige sweater, now had a design of many light colored Autumn leaves "knitted" into it! What an amazing sight!"

As she told her story, she seemed to remember, like it was only yesterday. Incidentally, the cat's name was Autumn!

Still today, Angela knows...*he's right here*. Although this may sound peculiar to some, it is Angela's summary of what she truly witnessed. It is important for us to believe in our hearts that our loved ones remain with us, despite the fact that we cannot see them. Therefore, I chose to include her experience in my writing for the benefit of anyone searching for answers or hoping to identify. Sometimes, there are no "sensible" answers, but they *do make sense to us, and that's all that matters!*

Yes....our loved ones are just beyond the horizon, loving us still and always near when we call upon them, as they are in praise and worship of our awesome God. He doesn't give us more than we can handle. I believe that is why He allows certain things to happen, which serve a purpose and help us to cope and carry on, as He gives us the necessary grace to bear our crosses and sometimes, just to put one foot in front of the other!

One day when my sister, Angela, was at the cemetery with me as we stood by Brendan's memorial stone, she commented about the Precious Moments Angels which I had placed there. I had bought a September angel with blue lettering printed across its bib and the angel was holding a small blue sapphire stone signifying its month. I had also bought a November angel, which was holding a small topaz stone and had matching lettering across its bib. Being very observant, she asked me if I had noticed anything about their eyes. Then she pointed out to me that the eyes of the November angel were looking down..."Brendan was born in November and he is looking down onto the earth," she said. Then she went on to say, "The eyes of the September angel are looking up into heaven and that's where he is now." I thought that was certainly very interesting, to say the least, and the fact that she even noticed how the eyes were focused! It's those little things that keep me believing. Someone greater than all of us is constantly intervening in our lives, giving us special little signs that really help us to believe, hope and wait upon the Lord.

One last account I would like to write about, refers to a

most amazing incident that occurred on New Year's Eve at about nine o'clock in the evening. I guess you might say it was Angela's last hurrah of the year 2009! Angela was at a friend's home caring for their daughter who was sound asleep in the next room. Arrangements had been made to spend the night and Angela was sitting up in bed with the pillows comfortably propped at her back, all set to watch one of her favorite television shows. She turned on the television set to watch her program, but after a few minutes, the picture was "snowy" accompanied by that annoying sound one hears when this happens. She started pushing the buttons on the television remote control expecting to correct the picture, but to no avail! Very frustrated, she asked herself, "Is it the wrong remote?" Nothing changed, no matter what she did as she tried to rectify the problem. She admitted she was feeling very desperate by this time.

"After half an hour of pushing buttons and being very frustrated," she explained, "I looked up and said----*Dad, Brendan, Uncle Dennis.....can somebody please help me fix this TV!!??* And, within thirty seconds, a perfectly clear picture appeared on the television screen!!"

Angela told me she couldn't believe what she was seeing and obviously was taken aback!

"Then," she said, "I looked up and all I could say was *thank you*!!" But that was just the beginning; she began to explain what happened next:

"About ten minutes later, as I was watching 'The Three Stooges,' all the overhead lights in the ceiling started flashing the color of bright orange! As best I can describe, it was like spotlights, alternately flashing bright orange lights, constantly, over a period of about three minutes!! I didn't know what to think! I just lay there totally dumbfounded; I couldn't believe my eyes! I know it was New Year's Eve, but I hadn't drunk any alcohol yet! I say this for the benefit of the reader who may have questioned me on that matter, so there it is!"

At this point in time, she admits she was definitely uneasy, but eventually, after she recovered from this very mysterious light-flashing incident, she courageously hopped out of bed to check the light switches and noticed they were off. Next, she turned the light switch on and clearly, the lights were white, not bright orange! She thought perhaps the lights were on a timer and were set to go off, but that wasn't the case either. It remained a mystery. Not knowing what to say in answer to all of this, she simply looked up and thought it might have been her loved ones' answer to her thanks for fixing the picture on the television set.

My immediate take on all of this was----*It is New Year's Eve, after all!* Brendan, our dad, and our Uncle Dennis were probably saying, "Happy New Year," complete with flashing lights, since perhaps, they were celebrating as well.

I remember thinking about Brendan this past New Year's Eve and how he enjoyed going to "First Night" with his friends. When my sister, Angela, told me about her startling and adventurous evening, it brought a smile to my face as I envisioned Brendan, my dad, my Uncle Dennis, and my husband's parents, Bob and Grace, all together bringing in the New Year. It helps me so very much when I see them together, because I can take a deep breath and feel that peace which surpasses all understanding.

Life is so unpredictable and so difficult sometimes, but I know the Lord is with us through it all and He wants to alleviate our burdens and lighten our load as we call on Him every day of our lives on this earth.

Chapter 28 - Peaceful Dove

For as long as I can remember, I have felt a personal connection to the image of the white dove and everything it stands for. Whenever any of my family makes his or her Confirmation, I feel especially inspired to attend, almost like something mystical or deeply spiritual is about to unfold. It's difficult to put into words, but the emotional component is a very great one, as I wait in expectant anticipation of something, not necessarily tangible, to happen for me personally. More often than not, I experience a kind of "inner healing," as the floodgates of peace open wide and enter my heart.

I have a small prayer card, that a friend of mine named Diane handed to me many years ago. Sketched on the card is a beautiful white dove, which appears to be coming down from the heavens. Beneath the dove are written these words:

Come Holy Spirit.....
Breathe in me, so I may know your presence,
Move in me, so I may do your will,
Live in me, so I may share your love.
Come Holy Spirit, Come... ...

It is just a simple prayer, but with inexplicable meaning for me and reciting it always gives me a warm, peaceful sense of comfort whenever my heart is restless. This prayer refreshes me in many ways.

When my husband and I chose the memorial stone for my son, Brendan, back in September of 2003, I knew I had to have a sketch of a dove on the stone. I searched and searched until I found the perfect dove to have sketched upon the front of his memorial stone.

We were provided with a very talented artist who did an excellent job of etching an image of a white dove flying towards the heavens, with the sun's rays filtering through the clouds in the skies just above. It had an incredibly peaceful image to it and we were tremendously grateful for her work. Very often, as I gaze upon the stone, deep in thought, and as I stand in front of Brendan's photograph adjacent to the dove, I can feel a very peaceful presence and I know "he's right here."

Ten months later on July 15, 2004, my beloved dad passed away. As I slowly and hesitantly entered the funeral home where my dad was being waked, I met my brother-in-law, Phil, who was standing in the hallway. I asked him: "Is he here?"

With a look of concern, he responded: "Is *who* here?" I knew my Dad *was* there, but it wasn't registering. It was too much to bear. I couldn't quite come to terms with his passing since I had lost my son just ten months earlier. Realizing I was in a fragile emotional state, my brother-in-law very gently said to me, "Yes, he's here," as I cautiously went inside. It was the grace of God working in my life during that extremely sad and difficult moment and I know the Lord Jesus literally walked beside me every step of the way into the room. It is times like these when I subconsciously reflect upon simple phrases of God's benevolent love, such as...."I am with you always," or.... "Faith promises to protect," and "Hold strong to the conviction of things not seen."

However, it was not until much later that I realized God was doing for me what I couldn't do for myself, for which I am very grateful. I love my dad so very much, however, this is no comparison to the love our Father in heaven has for him. At this time, the Lord chose to bring my father home to the heavens, freeing him from pain and unnecessary further suffering.

I believe the Lord said to my dad, "Well done my good and faithful servant. Enter now into the kingdom of heaven!!" Raising thirteen children, always with gentleness and compassion, was certainly no easy feat, but for both my parents, God was always the focal point in their lives. Therefore, I believe my dad was indeed blessed mightily by God and was greeted with open arms on that morning of July 15, 2004.

Four years later, a very dear cousin of my dad, named Lois, died on July 25, 2008, which was my dad's birthday. My mom and Lois had remained very close over the years. The wake was to be held at the same funeral home we attended when my dad died. I began to consider not attending this wake and funeral, since it would be at the exact same place, probably in the same room, where I had knelt before my father in dismay and disbelief. I prayed to God and of course, to my dad for discernment, strength and courage to make the right decision about this. In the meantime, it was assumed I was going, as I didn't share my feelings about this with anyone. Eventually, I did talk to my husband about it and he agreed to support me on whatever I decided, as he always does! I thank God every day for his genuine love.

The day of the wake arrived and I made the decision to attend with my husband. As we were walking toward the entrance of the funeral home, there was a little white dove in the flower garden! It certainly caught the attention of everyone who passed by! It was definitely very odd to encounter a pure white dove, very passively standing in the flower garden, unaffected by several people ambling by. I wondered where the dove came from. My initial assumption was, it must have some significant meaning for Lois. My thoughts were turned towards her and a possible connection with this dove. This kept me feeling completely calm as we made our way inside.

While inside, we looked at a video and reflected upon special moments during Lois' lifetime. I paid close attention to peoples' comments and asked if there was anything about a white dove that might have special meaning for Lois. Apparently, there was none. Still convinced there had to be something, I decided I would talk to her daughter about it later. Most importantly, I felt a peacefulness from within, as my focus was on this beautiful white dove, walking around the parking lot of the funeral home!

As we left for home, we noticed the dove was still there and again, discussed the peculiarity of it all.

The next morning, my husband and I briefly stopped by the funeral home before the service at Saint Peters Church, to leave the sympathy card I had forgotten the day before. As my husband went inside, I remained in the car and as I glanced across the street, there stood that same white dove! I was totally amazed it was still there. I grabbed for my camera and successfully took a photograph!

Later that morning, after the service, I still felt very strongly about talking to Lois' daughter about the white dove and was patiently waiting for the proper opportunity to discuss it. As I sat with my mom in deep discussion feeling almost obsessed about it, she explained, "I think the white dove was for you!" Suddenly, it all made sense! My prayers were answered and the presence of the beautiful, white dove undoubtedly helped to bring peace and calm to an otherwise emotionally-charged occasion that would have left me in turmoil.

About a week later, as my mom and I were still talking about the dove that greeted us when we arrived at the funeral home to attend Lois' wake, I asked her if she noticed the white dove on the back of Lois' memorial card. When she checked, she saw that there was no white dove on the back of her card, even though it was on the back of mine. This indeed, was another mysterious sign of the power of The Holy Spirit, symbolized by the white dove.

I often talk to my dad in the heavens and as I was looking at his memorial card, I noticed on the front of it, there was a *white dove* flying free into the heavens. On the back is written the verse,

"I'm Free."

I know deep within the confines of my heart, my dad is with me whenever I need him, always close in ways I will never understand but will always believe, beyond the shadow of a doubt. Yes, he's right here.

My dad always had a special devotion to the Blessed Mother. Interestingly, in a book written by Louis Kaczmarek entitled "The Wonders She Performs," there is frequent mention of white doves nestling at the feet of the statue of Our Lady of Fatima. Wherever the Pilgrim Virgin statue was escorted, Kaczmarek remarks, "White doves miraculously appeared." Of special significance to me are the following words to a well-known prayer, The Apostles Creed:

...And in Jesus Christ, his only son, our Lord, "who was conceived by the Holy Spirit, born of the Virgin Mary..." The Holy Spirit, the *spouse* of the Virgin Mary is represented by *white doves hovering* or *protecting* the Blessed Mother. This all resonated with me as a simple explanation.

Soothing music to my soul are the words to the beautiful song, "Hail Mary: Gentle Woman."

"Gentle woman, quiet light, morning star, so strong and bright, gentle Mother, peaceful *dove,* teach us wisdom; teach us love."

These beautiful words permeate my soul as I look upon our Blessed Mother, the mother of us all, here on earth and as Queen of Heaven.

In May of 2004, while attending a seminar on "Inner Healing," I read these words on the front of a prayer card written in gold printing, alongside a white dove:

"As the bird, free of its cage, seeks the heights, so the Christian soul, in death, flies home to God."

This prayer card captures the vision of a *white dove*, flying towards the bright rays of the sun, peering through the clouds.

Written on the back of the card are the words to a well-known poem written in 1932 by Mary Elizabeth Frye, "Do Not Stand At My Grave And Weep."

It has certainly taken me a long while to agree with the wording of this poem because for so long my heart was shattered, broken and I couldn't get past the heartache and pain. The roadblocks of hesitation and uncertainty prevented me from trusting in God completely even though I knew I had absolutely no control. I had a really difficult time with this concept, especially after the unexpected loss of my son, Brendan and the death of my beloved father ten months later. After having been challenged in numerous ways, I eventually began to place my trust in God completely, and the healing process began, slowly but surely. I was told over and over, "Be gentle with yourself," but that, too, was a long road ahead and just the beginning. Today, I can truly thank God because I realize He has **always** been my pillar of strength and is in complete control, making life much simpler. Therefore, I can write with truth in my heart and a dawning of new hope, the words to this poem:

> *"Do not stand at my grave and weep*
> *I am not there. I do not sleep.*
> *I am a thousand winds that blow.*
> *I am a diamond glint on snow.*
> *I am the sunlight on ripened grain.*
> *I am the gentle autumn rain.*
> *When you awake in the morning hush,*
> *I am the swift up flinging rush,*
> *Of quiet birds in circling flight.*
> *I am the soft star shine at night.*
> *Do not stand by my grave and cry.*
> *I am not there. I did not die.*
> ***I live with the Risen Lord"***

Seven years later, as I reflect upon this poem, I truly *feel* Brendan and my dad's love all around me and I feel peace and serenity in my heart.

After reflecting upon the inspiring words of this poem, I continue to visit them at the cemetery, talk to them or say a little prayer as I experience their loving presence. Each time I am there, I look into the beautiful blue skies, feel the gentle breezes, and notice the birds in the trees or the little rabbits hopping by, as I take time to listen to the quiet peacefulness all around me.

Chapter 29 - Fragrance of Incense

Although this may sound peculiar, after my son, Brendan, passed away, both my husband and I could often detect a hint of wood burning, as we were riding along in our car. Our first assumption was that someone was burning leaves in their yard, but when we looked for evidence, we didn't see anyone. Sometimes, only I could detect it, and at other times, it was just my husband. He would "sniff the air," and ask if I could smell anything, which I could not. Unfortunately, we rarely detected the "wood burning scent," at the same time. We discussed the possibility of someone burning wood in their fireplace or we looked again for evidence of someone raking and burning leaves in their yard. There was never a clear cut answer.

Whatever the case may be, my husband and I both believed this scent was a sign of Brendan's presence, because it all began after our son was gone and at unexpected moments. We had never heard of such a thing, but my husband and I concluded it was our son, letting us know he was with us in spirit. Even though we couldn't "see" him, we definitely "felt" his presence during those moments. Also, it was not unusual for us to see a Chevy Blazer drive by, right when one of us detected the scent of the wood burning! (Brendan was driving a Blazer at the time of his accident). However, we never discussed this with anyone, since we had no reason to do so; it was a private matter we kept to ourselves...until now!

Recently, I thought about how Brendan liked to burn incense sticks while he was studying or listening to music, and his room would often have a pleasant aroma of various scents of incense. I, too, enjoyed the scent and would often light them myself, something I did for relaxation. Still today, whenever I burn an incense stick, I think of Brendan, especially since it was something he often put on his Christmas list. Maybe Brendan figured I would put this all together, which is certainly a possible explanation.

As you read the following incident, perhaps you will agree, there is something mysterious, yet worth mentioning, about this "fragrance of incense".

It was 9:10 AM., and the Mass had just begun. As I stood and listened to the priest say the opening prayers, I thought I detected a faint, but distinctive odor of incense in the air. For a brief moment, I decided it was just a lingering aroma in the church and dismissed it from my mind. Then, it became even stronger and the fragrance of burning incense permeated the air all around me. I began to question if there was a fire starting somewhere, but as I looked around, no one else seemed the least bit concerned about this strong scent of incense! For a moment, I wondered if the aroma was coming from the candles in the adoration chapel. This thought, however, was fleeing and short-lived, as I soon realized that the door to the entrance of the chapel was closed. As I breathed in the air around me, trying not to look too conspicuous, I experienced a "tingling sensation" entering through my nostrils and into my sinuses, as the aroma of incense became stronger! Again, thoughts began to run through my head: doesn't anyone else smell this? Why does no one else seem concerned? As I observed the priest, he continued offering the Mass as usual. At this point, I realized that this mysterious aroma of incense obviously had a special significance for me alone.

I glanced at my watch just because time and dates always seem to have a special significance, or an important connection to a meaningful happening in my life. At that moment, I noticed it was *9:11 A.M.* Brendan passed away on *September 11,* 2003, seven years ago. Then I knew for sure that Brendan was there with me at that precise moment. I *felt* his presence, very strongly, and *heard* him saying, "I'm right here, Mom; I'm never far away." I closed my eyes, enjoying his presence until the scent of the incense dissipated, while saying over and over again, "I love you, I love you, I love you so much."

The timing of this occurrence was quite amazing as this all happened in early September, just before our annual fundraiser for the music scholarship fund we had planned for September 12, 2010. I had been thinking of Brendan a lot, as I always do during this time of year when our family and friends come together to share our loving memories and dedicate the day to him. We thank God this scholarship fund has become a wonderfully successful music program for the students at the elementary school in Rochester. Perhaps Brendan wanted me to know he is very happy for the youngsters, who benefit from this wonderful program. Once again, it's clear to me, he's right here!

After my mother-in-law died, I sometimes detected the scent of her wind song cologne, while sitting in the church pew at Saint Rose of Lima Church where we had often sat together at the five o'clock Mass. This morning, I am reminded of that incidence, as I sit here at Saint Francis Xavier Church and detect this scent of incense. Brendan was very close to his grandmother and was devastated when she passed away in her sleep on October 1, 1997, just six years previously to his own passing. I know they are together in the heavens today.

Perhaps this sort of thinking sounds peculiar and out of the ordinary to some, but for me it is very real and it resonates with every beat of my heart. It is not meant to convince the reader that he or she needs to agree with me; it is simply to describe my deeply personal experience and part of my story, of how everything fits together. My experience may not necessarily fit together *immediately,* but when the truth is revealed, I feel serene and at peace.

After sitting in silence with the Lord, praying and discerning about a situation, the answer may come very spontaneously into my mind, several hours or even days later. It may be when I awake the following morning, or whenever the Holy Spirit chooses to speak to me; it's as though a light comes on, and the answer flashes across my mind, or I hear the words in my head. In any event, the answer becomes clear!

Chapter 30 - Pennies From Heaven

This title may sound silly to some, but for me, it speaks the truth. It all began very soon after my son, Brendan was no longer with us. Love never dies and time after time he has let me know he is "just beyond that veil." I know I will see him again in the heavenly realm and how incredible that will be, so I wait in faith and trust, with God's abundant graces, always giving me everything I need. I know today that my finding pennies was perhaps Brendan's gentle, playful way of getting my attention and strengthening my trust and faith in God.

As I mentioned earlier in my book, my husband and I were staying with my daughter and son-in-law at the time of Brendan's accident. We had planned to stay with them until the completion of our new home. I thank God we were all together during that period of our lives and will be forever grateful for our strong family bond we always shared. My daughter, Lisa, lost her little brother and there are really no words to describe her pain, yet she had the strength and courage that was beyond incredible to minister to my needs as well as her own. The Lord knew we would need each other's company and support during this time that he provided. Some days, I spent hours at a time sitting in my quiet space, when I needed time alone. She would come upstairs and offer me a cup of peppermint tea. It is moments like these that I realize the Lord's greatness and goodness, to have given me such a thoughtful, compassionate daughter, whose heart was full of love and understanding. She gave me permission to grieve in my own way, regardless of what she thought about it; she was always respectful of my needs.

Eventually, I knew I needed to persuade myself to go outside and take a leisurely walk. In my heart, I knew Brendan was urging me to do this. My final words to him, on September 11, 2003 were, "I'll see you later, Brendan; I'm going for my walk." I know that he answered me, but to this day, I can't remember his exact words. I remember looking at him in the garage, putting things away after he had just washed his Chevy Blazer, his pride and joy. I will **never forget** that moment. Little did I know the scenario that would follow.

Then it all began and I found pennies everywhere I walked. The thought of "pennies from heaven" would ring in my head! I began to collect and save them, while putting them in a special place, believing Brendan was giving me a hug each time I found one and he knew that I knew. I played little games in my head, so I would feel better. Interestingly, it's not that I went out *looking* for pennies, but they found me! Then, of course I would think of Brendan and feel a personal connection to him. Any parent who has experienced the heartache that accompanies being separated from his or her child, by a sudden, unexpected death, probably will understand.

Some weeks later, I clearly remember walking into a small store, and upon entering, I spotted a penny on the ground, which I quickly scooped up and placed in my pocket. By the look on my face, one would have thought it was something of much greater value, but for me it was a treasure of a much greater kind! With a smile on my face, I took a deep breath as I immediately thought of Brendan. It was as if he were right there next to me at that very moment. As the cashier handed me my change of three dollars and *one cent*, I couldn't help but chuckle to myself as I remembered an incident that happened several years earlier when Brendan and I were there at this same variety store.

It was a beautiful sunny day. Brendan and I happened to be traveling together that day and he had stopped here to fill up his gas tank. Brendan went inside to pay, and a few minutes later, came out the door looking quite annoyed. Brendan had always *tried* to be patient, but on this particular day, he surely was put to the test! He asked me, "Do you have two cents? I can't believe it…The lady at the cash register insists on the *two cents!*" I didn't have the two pennies, but I did have a nickel which I gave to him. Seconds later, I decided to go inside to see why this lady was giving Brendan so much grief. I guess it's the protectiveness we mothers feel for our children even as they become adults. A few moments later, as we walked to his car, we had a good laugh for ourselves, realizing how trivial it all was.

Looking back now, I realize how moments such as these, safely tucked away in my bank of memories, have become very special ones. Little flashbacks, such as this, will always put a smile on my face as I think of Brendan today, seven years later. How I appreciate every one of them, regardless of how silly or insignificant it may have been. Today, every memory remains precious. Truly, "it's the little things that mean a lot!"

On my first day of returning to work in late January, I spotted a shiny, new penny on the ground as I opened the door of my car. Then, lying on the floor directly in front of my locker, was another shiny penny! As I picked it up and looked at it, I read, "2003" and immediately, I thought of Brendan. Somehow, I *knew* he was with me saying, "I'm right here! Everything is going to be okay, Mom. It's going to be a good day..." and it was!

Time went by, and I continued finding pennies... everywhere! Whenever my husband and I go on vacation, we always find time to go on our walks. Early in March of 2010, we spent a few days visiting friends in West Palm Beach, Florida. We decided to take a walk around the condominiums near where we were staying. During the course of our walk, we spotted seven pennies in various locations along our way. Both my husband and I were laughing by the time we had found the seventh one! It was indeed our lucky day! (we know the number seven means completion). I said to my husband, "I guess that's it for today! Isn't it amazing how something so simple, can be so exciting!" Again, it's the little things that mean a lot!

On another occasion, one beautiful, sunny afternoon, early in the month of June, my husband and I took advantage of the glorious weather, as we got ready to plant flowers around our son's memorial stone, as we do every year. Just a short distance from the cemetery, I had seen an outdoor display of various assortments of flowering plants for sale. There I was, amongst a variety of gorgeous plants, trying to decide what I wanted to bring to the cemetery! After about half an hour of looking around, I found myself standing in front of a beautiful, healthy-looking, purple-flowered plant with bright green leaves, which I had been admiring and had put aside as one of my possible choices. It was called a "dark lavender African daisy." As I stooped down to examine it more closely, I spotted a penny next to this beautiful potted plant! Wow! All I could say was, "Oh my gosh!! Thank you, Brendan! Now I know for sure, this is the one I will plant at the cemetery!"

Today, on this 27th day of August, the lovely daisies are still blossoming, its leaves are still fresh and green, and it remains absolutely beautiful! I recently took a photo, not only to capture its beauty, but as a special reminder of this precious moment. I'll look at it and hear Brendan's soft-spoken voice say to me, once again…..."I'm right here, Mom. I'm always with you."

Just a couple weeks ago, as I arrived at a meeting, I was greeted by a friend of mine. She smiled at me and handed me a penny. She said, "I found a penny on my dashboard. I never find pennies anywhere! When I saw you pull up next to me, I knew it was for you!" About a week earlier, I had shared with her, in a heart-to-heart conversation, the very special significance of finding pennies since Brendan's accident and what a great comfort that has been for me. When Mary Ellen handed me the penny, I thought of Brendan. In my heart, I heard him say…"I'm right here!"

As I alluded to earlier in this story, the number seven indicates completeness and it also means spiritual perfection. This was a meeting that Brendan had regularly attended with me each week, for a period of seven years, seven months, and seven days. This is certainly something to think about. Now, as I am writing this book, it dawns on me that he has been gone for seven years. His journey on this earth was complete at twenty-seven years of age. Still, I think about him every day, while looking forward to finding more "pennies from heaven."

The appearance of pennies continued. One afternoon, my daughter, Lisa, myself, and her three boys, stopped at Friendly's for an ice cream. I couldn't help but reminisce about the afternoon of September 11, 2003; On that day, Brendan had brought his nephew Brendan (his namesake), here for an ice cream treat and won for him a Patrick doll. (This was a character from the television program, "Sponge Bob"). Trying to stay focused on the happy memories, I watched Vincent, (Brendan's cousin) now eleven years old, putting forth his best effort, positive attitude and intense concentration, attempting to grasp hold of a stuffed animal in the glass display case. "Wow… Uncle Brendan must have been really good at this," he said. "This is really hard!" There at his side, were his younger brothers, Nicholas and Luke, with their wide-eyed anticipation, cheering him on. Deciding to try again later, we all went outside to enjoy our ice cream cones!

Just as we were about to leave, there it was! I called out to my daughter, "Lisa, I found a penny! That's so cool, since we're also, at a Friendly's today." It was a wonderful thing; I felt so elated, and my day was complete. I knew Brendan was there with us as I held the penny in my hand and smiled. And I heard a little echo in my heart saying to me, "I'm right here, Mom; Keep smiling."

My husband and I recently returned home from a sixteen day pilgrimage to Portugal, Spain and France, of which another book could be written, describing our incredible experience. All throughout our trip, we knew Brendan was definitely with us. On day fourteen, as I stood up to exit the tour bus, I noticed Brendan's photo lying on my seat. Somehow, it had fallen out of a book I had been reading. As I turned to pick it up, I spotted a two cent euro coin, barely visible, peaking through the cushion of the seat, and I said to my husband, "One cent for each of us!" We laughed, as we both knew we would eventually find at least one penny during the course of our visit. Then we agreed, once again, Brendan had been with us all the while. We just looked at each other and smiled, since it was understood…. "He's right here."

You see, it doesn't really matter where we are…..We believe Brendan is *always* with us, no matter how far, no matter how near.

Chapter 31 - As One Door Closes

At the age of five, I clearly remember accompanying my mother to where she worked as a registered nurse. On that day, a very great impression was made upon my life. As we walked through the entranceway of the room at the top of the stairs, I vividly recall seeing a frail old woman, lying in a bed in the far corner of the room. As I glanced at her face, her eyes spoke to my soul, and my heart was filled with compassion as we walked towards her. As we stood at her bedside, she smiled at me as my mom introduced me to her, and she held her hand out to me….a vivid flashback of yesteryear! Although I was quite young, it was a moment of truth for me, as I said to my mom with words of conviction,

"When I grow up, I want to be a nurse… just like you," and so it was. My dream became a reality, and for forty three years, my career as a nurse was rewarding and fulfilling, as I cared for patients in various areas of nursing, including medical-surgical, neurological intensive care, and orthopedics.

November of 1986 marked the beginning of the years spent working in maternity, which I enjoyed so very much, and remained there for the next twenty four years until my nursing career was brought to completion. During that time period, following September of 2003 with the death of my youngest son, Brendan, my world turned upside down. It was definitely a struggle returning to work after being away for a period of five months, but I knew the time had not yet come to make any major changes. Deep down inside I knew the Lord would carry me through and I was given the courage and strength to take one day at a time, with the help of my friends at work. Somehow, I knew God had a plan and a purpose for my life, although I found it exceedingly difficult to understand what this might be. Then, during the next seven years, His plan became clearer to me, and with His grace I was able to identify with and tenderly care for other grieving parents who had experienced the unexpected loss of their baby, still in the womb.

My heart remembers an incident when I was in the

company of an expectant mom overcome with grief, when the usual, pleasant and familiar sound of her baby's heartbeat from the monitor, was replaced by an unexpected silence. During these moments of desperate shock and disbelief, I could sit with her as she sobbed uncontrollably in this nightmare of deep sorrow. I could hear the words echoing in my own head… "How can this be happening?!" Circumstances may have differed but the pain was equally as great. My heart truly felt her heart-wrenching pain and suffering, and I could say to her with all sincerity, "I know how you feel; I'm so very sorry." I believe we are here on this earth to comfort those who are hurting, especially during those times our personal experience can benefit them.

During those difficult moments when I wanted to express my heartfelt condolences to a grieving couple filled with total despair, I always thought of Brendan, as I heard his still small voice clearly saying to me: "I love you Mom…I'm right here." These encouraging thoughts gave me whatever I needed to quietly minister to a heartbroken couple…a time when the heart speaks volumes and no words are necessary.

As time continued, I thankfully experienced many more happy and healthy births of which my heart will treasure and remember. Today, I feel honored every time a young girl thanks me for the help I provided during her labor and delivery experience, or immediately after her baby's birth, as I placed her precious newborn into her loving arms! Throughout the years, the miracle of birth never ceased to amaze me! Truly, however, I owe it all to the honor and glory of God, since He is my guiding light and walks with me every day of my life; of this I have no doubt! The joy of witnessing new life entering this world is one I will remember forever, including the births of my four grandsons, Vincent, Brendan, Nicholas and Luke!

Sometime during the year of 2008, I knew in my heart the time had come to close that chapter of my life as a nurse. With the advancement of computer technology, nursing practice was rapidly changing. I believed strongly, the Lord was leading me to bigger and better things, that there is a time and reason for everything, and now was that time. The decision was made to take an early retirement which I did with absolutely no regrets! I also

133

knew the Lord was calling me to write this book, an inspiration put on my heart, several months before my final decision to retire. Over the years, I had kept several journals and had written about very meaningful experiences which enabled me to put one foot in front of the other. Now, I believed was the time to share these experiences with other parents who lost a child, regardless of the age or circumstances. Quite as importantly, I wanted to help them, to perhaps learn more about the reality of eternal life.

I would like to share the following words of encouragement written in a condolence card I received, after the untimely passing of my son, Brendan:

"A Word of Consolation"

"If a tiny baby could think, it would be afraid of birth. To leave the only world it had known would seem a kind of death. But immediately after birth the child finds itself in loving arms, showered with affection and cared for at every moment.

Passing through death is really a birth into a new and better world. For those who are left behind, let not your hearts grieve, as if there were no hope. Life is changed, not taken away. Our dear ones live on, in a world beautiful beyond anything we can imagine. There they await the day when they will welcome us with joy!"

Oftentimes, this short reading helps to remind me to "feel that joy," although, not always an easy task, obviously because I miss my son, Brendan, so very much.

Just today, as I sat in my car parked at the cemetery, my eyes glued to the framed photo of Brendan on the front of his memorial stone, once again, the stark reality "hit" me, but then instead, I saw his smile and the sun shining brightly on his handsome face, and it was like he was saying to me,

"Mom, Don't be sad; I'm right here with you." And as strange as this may sound, I saw him smiling back at me.

Soon afterwards as I sat in my car, I randomly opened my Bible and read these words: "Praise the Lord, O my soul; all my inmost being, praise his holy name." (Psalm 103:1).

Immediately, I recalled a conversation I had had with Brendan, on September11, 2003 as he was washing his Chevy Blazer, when during our conversation, I had said to him, "Praise God!" With a very positive response, Brendan raised his arm in the air and exclaimed, "Yeah!"

Also, of special significance to me was the number 103. Brendan had received his training as a telecommunications technician from local union 103 in Boston. Within the next five minutes, I felt as though I just had a conversation with him. I felt uplifted, joyful, and refreshed.

I was inspired to phone my husband, and ten minutes later, we were raking leaves and cleaning up the pine needles on the ground as we commented how Brendan loved this type of landscape work. We both knew he was enjoying the time the three of us were spending together. Our hearts felt at peace again! These are the little things that mean so much and help us to feel his constant presence and a song echoes in our hearts….. "Till We Meet Again."

As time continued, I started to look forward to that wonderful day of freedom when I would retire, and have the opportunity to actually write my first book.

One morning while at work, my good friend, Donna Messia came into the nursery to discuss a retirement party that was being planned and wanted to be sure that the possible date would be feasible with my schedule. Then she tactfully began to explain to me….

"We thought we would have you take a look at the menu to decide upon a few choices, since it is your night. Some of the girls thought you might get upset when you read one of the choices on the menu and they considered deleting it! I explained I would discuss it with you ….so here it is!"

She looked at me with a smile on her face and handed me the menu that she pulled from behind her back. I quickly glanced at this "mystery menu" and read…. *Saint Brendan Pot Pie!* How awesome was that! I gave Donna a big hug and couldn't thank her enough for professing her faith in me since she knew, contrary to the general opinion, I would be ecstatic about this choice. I will be forever grateful to her for standing in my defense! Then Donna

135

said to me, "Another chapter for your book," to which I quickly and laughingly agreed! We both knew it was definitely not a coincidence, and we looked at each other and said together, with our voices in sync, "He's right here!" I believe Brendan wanted to say, "Congratulations on your retirement, Mom" and he was absolutely, beyond a shadow of a doubt, right there by my side.

February 27, 2010 was my final day working as a nurse. My husband and I had our bags packed and ready to fly out to West Palm Beach, Florida the next day! We had purchased airplane tickets several months earlier, as a celebration to mark the beginning of our retirement together and another chapter of our lives.

Bright and early the next morning, we went to the cemetery to give the grounds some last-minute pampering before our departure to the airport. Before we left, I stooped down to kiss Brendan's framed photo mounted on his memorial stone even though I knew he would be with us in spirit throughout the trip. Yes, his love is eternal; his love has no boundaries! God's promise of eternal life fills us with hope beyond measure and we know we will be together one day for all eternity! Praise God! As my husband and I were driving through the cemetery, I "heard" the innocent little voice of my grandson, Nicholas, saying, "It's not really him, Gramma; It's just his picture!" I certainly cherish the truths that come out of the mouths of little children and how we can learn from them! The sweet sound of his voice brought a smile to my face! I thank God every single day for my grandchildren, my greatest treasures!

A couple of hours later, my husband and I had arrived at the airport, checked our baggage and were about to receive our boarding passes. As the lady behind the ticket counter handed them to us, she courteously said, "Boarding will begin at 9:11." Immediately, I looked at my husband and smiled. We both knew Brendan was saying to us in his loving, caring fashion, "I'm right here." (September 11th was the date of his passing).

Just a few minutes later, as I placed my carry-on luggage into the bin on the conveyor belt, there was a bright, shiny penny, lying at my feet on the carpet in front of me. "Ahh," I thought to myself, "Brendan's here! Thanks, Brendan!" I picked it up and tucked it safely into my pocket, feeling very reassured of his loving presence and off we went to our designated gate. Upon our arrival, we were informed there had been a change and boarding would be at "gate 26." This was another subtle reminder of Brendan's presence being with us, since he was born on November 26th! We arrived in perfect time, as boarding for our row had already begun. We hustled down the aisle towards our seats, 8E and 8F. We noticed it definitely was a full flight as we watched the large number of passengers quickly filing in and taking their assigned seats. After everyone was apparently seated, much to my surprise I noticed *no one* was sitting in seat *8D*, beside my husband. I smiled and said to him, "I'll bet no one sits in this seat because it's for Brendan." Somehow we both knew this! Then I looked at the *penny* I had slipped into my pocket earlier and noted the year imprinted was *2008*! I chuckled to myself as I heard Brendan say, *"Just in case you haven't got it yet, I'm right here!!"*

Waiting for takeoff, I turned on the music channel and Bryan Adams was singing these words: "Everything I do, I do it for you." Tears filled my eyes; it was song number 23, and I thought to myself, "March 23rd is my birthday." I closed my eyes and while listening to the words, I felt my son near me as I do so often, especially during those times when I want to reach out and touch him and feel his gentle hug. It appears to me that the more aware I become of what the Lord wants to reveal to me, the more is revealed. It's all about faith, trust and total surrender to the promise of God's incredible love and mercy.

As time continues, I look forward to a future filled with many new and wonderfully exciting experiences, as I wait in joyful anticipation.

Chapter 32 - Splendor in the Sky

It was three o'clock in the afternoon. The weather had been cloudy all day with a chance of showers in the forecast. As my husband and I walked down the driveway to plant the Christmas tree that had been beautifully decorated at the cemetery, we realized it was beginning to sprinkle a light mist of rain, which soon developed into a light shower! Only about ten minutes earlier, just as my husband had finished digging the hole where we had decided to plant the tree, the sun began to shine! We were delighted and had commented what a perfect day it was to plant this beautiful spruce tree! As I held my arms out to let the rain fall gently upon the palms of my hands, I said with expectant anticipation… "The sun is shining and it's raining, so that means there's going to be a rainbow!" Just after I said this, we both looked up, and to our amazement, we saw in the sky, an absolutely beautiful rainbow in the shape of a perfect semi-circle over our house!! It seemed to get brighter by every second! Our hearts were filled with an incredible sense of joy and awe as we said together, almost simultaneously, "Brendan's here!" We both could *feel* his warmth and love pouring down upon us from the sky above! It was almost like we could see Brendan, himself, calling out to us, "I'm right here!! I'm never far from you!! And, by the way, what a perfect place you chose to plant the tree!" It was such a moment of joy for us, a combination of a Christmas gift and an exultation of "Happy New Year!"

    I immediately ran inside the house to get my camera so I could take a photograph! When I returned, I noticed the brightness of the rainbow was already beginning to dim and the clouds were slowly returning trying to block the sunshine. I took several pictures all within seven minutes. As the rainbow was fading away, my husband shouted, "Thank you Brendan!!" Then, ten minutes later to be exact, the rainbow was gone and the clouds returned and a fog began to roll in. It was a glorious moment in time and one we will treasure forever! My husband described the incident perfectly the next day when he said to our friend, Dave, "I felt tingly all over!"

One might think my imagination is running wild, but today happens to be the wonderful feast of the Epiphany, also called, "Little Christmas." This is when the three kings saw "a star of wonder" in the night skies and were led to the Infant Jesus in Bethlehem, where they brought him their gifts of gold, frankincense and myrrh. We, too, were gifted with a rainbow in the sky; a beautiful gift, filled with the promise of Brendan's presence with us on *this* day, as we prepared to plant the memorial tree in *his* honor, as we do each year. It was exactly what we both needed at the culmination of the Christmas season.

Earlier in the day, before taking the decorations off the tree, still placed at the cemetery, I hesitated for a few minutes and thought to myself, "Is it really seven years since he's been gone? How can that be possible?" Sometimes, I wish I could just stop time, and gently capture all the very special memories from the years past, and quietly float away for just a little while and allow myself to get lost in this bubble of timeless memories! What a wonderful opportunity it would be, to relive them before having to rush into the New Year once again!! Perhaps it is another good reason to write this book and one day I will have the opportunity to look back over the years and smile.

I believe the Lord also sends special unexpected moments of joy and laughter during the holiday season, to help soften the very sad and sometimes difficult moments many experience during this emotionally-charged time of year. However, I know for certain the Lord doesn't give us more than we can handle.

For example, my heart experienced a very tender moment at Mass this morning when we sang the words to the "Irish Melody," a song which was played at Brendan's funeral Mass. I just stood there feeling unprepared and dumbfounded, as a lump settled in my throat. No one knew the tenderness of that moment, but the Lord did and I believe Brendan did as well. I definitely felt him standing by my side, saying to me, "You can do it Mom, I know you can," and that is precisely how Brendan carries me through moments like these. Little did I know then, what was about to happen approximately five hours later, when my husband and I had the awesome experience of seeing the beautiful rainbow encircling our house!

As a confirmation and a reminder of his presence on this day of January 2, 2011, we believe Brendan sent us sunshine, a rain shower, and a rainbow all during the fifteen minutes we spent outside planting his memorial tree! Coincidence? We say, absolutely not! A God-incidence? We say definitely yes!!

As an added bonus, this all happened at three o'clock, also known as The Hour of Divine Mercy. This is a very special time of day when many people are praying the Chaplet all over the world, whether it is at three o'clock in the morning or three o'clock in the afternoon. Oftentimes, at this hour I will also stop to pray for all those I love, and remind myself to trust in Jesus, who is merciful and faithful all the time. Then I hear Brendan say to me with reassurance, *"Keep your eyes fixed on Jesus."* These quiet words that I hear in my heart, really help me to stay focused as I gain the serenity to accept the things I cannot change and trust completely in Jesus, Who always lovingly and compassionately hears and answers all our prayers.

Fifteen days later on the 17th of January, while I was attending morning Mass, the words to the entrance antiphon immediately caught my attention. I *knew* it was important to conclude this story of my book with these words from psalm 92, verses 12 and 13:

"The just man will flourish like the palm tree. Planted in the courts of God's house, he will grow great like the cedars of Lebanon."

In my heart, I was thinking of Brendan and about the memorial tree my husband and I had planted a couple weeks earlier--timing is everything! I felt Brendan reassuring me, "I am in God's house." A stream of tears flooded my eyes as he seemed so near to me, reconfirming what I already believed. For those of us here on earth, we can admire the beauty of the spruce tree we planted, as it continues to grow strong and tall. In the quiet, we can hear Brendan say... "I'm right here!"

Then as Mass continued and I stood for the gospel reading, my eyes focused upon these words:

"Alleluia! The word of God is living and effective, able to discern reflections and thoughts of the heart. Alleluia!"

Somehow, I *knew* my God was speaking to me, personally,

confirming what I had just read. I felt God's love and compassion saying to me, "Yes, Brendan is with me, but he is also with you, just as I am with you....always." These words had profound meaning and were absorbed into my heart. Sitting before the Blessed Sacrament after Mass, the words to the song, "Glory and Praise to Our God," rang out in my head. I felt such joy and peace in my heart...

    ..."*Glory and praise to our God, who alone gives light to our days. Many are the blessings he bears to those who trust in his ways.*"

    God is so good and is profoundly faithful! I have found over the years when I've needed Him the most, as I take one step towards Him, He takes ten steps towards me and wraps his arms around me with His unconditional, abiding love, protection and grace. He gives me the strength to carry on, one day at a time. Yes, God's love *does* cast out all fear! The Lord doesn't give us more than we can handle because he always gives us the grace and the strength to get through difficult times. Most often, I find my answers in The Word of God, the greatest book ever written, where God speaks to us personally.

Chapter 33 - Another Priceless Gift

On the evening of March 19, 2011, seven and one half years after Brendan's passing, something amazing happened. My husband and I were at a dinner function at our parish church at Saint Rose of Lima. Six months had passed since we had last seen Vicki's parents, Paul and Janet. (At the time of Brendan's accident, he and Vicki were engaged). It was wonderful to see them there and to catch up on all the news. We talked for quite a while about the indescribable joys of grandparenthood. Their little grandson was a year old already, keeping Vicki and her husband, Michael, quite busy.

At the end of the evening, Paul gently informed me he had an audio clip of Brendan's voice, as he left a message on the answering machine for Vicki. He asked if I was interested in having the recording forwarded to my email. Although I had mixed emotions as to how it might affect me, I knew I wanted to hear Brendan's voice again, so I decided to take the chance and accept his offer. Then I exclaimed,

"It's my birthday in four days! Brendan always figures some way to send me a birthday gift! As usual, his timing is perfect! I'll be right back!"

Then I scurried off to find a pen to write down my email address for Paul. I felt incredibly happy and excited, as I looked forward to the opportunity to actually hear Brendan's voice, after seven long years.

"I'll send it tonight," Paul said. I was overflowing with gratitude and appreciation.

Later that evening, I sat down in front of my computer and read these words:

"Hi Maggie, The audio clip is an attachment. Just double click the file and it should play. The date of this file is Wednesday, September 03, 2003, 1039:13 AM. Take care, Paul."

I took a deep breath; I realized this date was just eight days before Brendan's fatal car accident. As I held Brendan's photo in my hands, I listened to the recording of his kind, considerate, compassionate tone of voice. I closed my eyes and listened, again and again, over and over to the sound of Brendan's voice. It was as if he was sitting there beside me. I didn't want to move a muscle. His gentleness, his warmth and his love enveloped me. A beautiful peacefulness flowed through me. I wanted it to last forever. I knew in my heart this was indeed, *my birthday gift from Brendan.* I *felt* him say, "I'm right here, Mom. Happy Birthday! I love you!"

On the following day, I received a second email from Paul, which confirmed and validated Brendan's presence, as I read,

"I'm so happy that I found that audio clip and was able to send it to you to enjoy. A strange thing happened last night when I was typing your email address in the 'to:' section of the email. I started to type "mmc" and the computer completed the rest of your email address (gee@verizon.net) without me typing it. This only happens when I have already placed someone in my address book. I did not have your email address until last night. Very strange! This has never happened before. When I checked my address book, your email address was there! How could it have gotten there unless you and I had corresponded in the past? To the best of my knowledge, we have never exchanged emails. I have no idea how this happened.....God bless, Paul."

I truly believe it is no coincidence that I received this "gift" just four days before my birthday. I also believe it was no coincidence my husband and I met up with Paul and Janet on that evening. We don't always know why certain things happen at a certain moment in time, and although this entire experience is beyond all our human understanding, I believe it was Divine Intervention. Years later, we may begin to see how all things work together for our good. God always knows what we need when we need it. Yes, God is always faithful; I will hold onto that truth, for I believe it is the only explanation! Thank you, Jesus!

Chapter 34 - Walk Down Memory Lane

From the time he was a young boy, people would say to me, *"There's something special about Brendan."* I always thought this to be true, but to hear this said by others, who perhaps had only known him for just a short while, was confirmation and it always brought a smile to my face. His generous and caring ways of taking the time to listen or help someone in any way he could, were just a few of his positive attributes. He had a loving heart of gold and was loved and admired in return by infinitely many people, including friends and family.

After his tragic and unexpected loss, I received heartfelt messages of love, one by one, as I was presented with innumerable cards, letters, phone calls, visits, and prayers, for the days, weeks, and months to follow.

I would like to share these beautiful words of poetry engraved on the hearts of Brendan's cousins, aunt and godson. These poems were proudly presented to me in Brendan's honor.

The first poem was written by Brendan's thirteen year old cousin, Danielle Wedge, the daughter of my youngest sister, Cecelia and her husband, John.

"Only God Knows Why"

I'll tell you a story
Of my cousin I once had;
Thinking of this person
Only makes me sad.
I knew he loved me
Because he told me so,
But why God had to take his life
...Only God will know.
I was going to school
When I heard of his death;
I began to cry
And I couldn't catch my breath.
As I walked to his casket
To say a little prayer,
I whispered to myself
Have a peaceful rest.
I asked why he had to go
Why he had to die
I thought I heard him whisper back...
"ONLY GOD KNOWS WHY"

"Brendan, we love you and miss you lots. You will forever live on in our hearts*"

These beautiful words of love, forever to be treasured are encased in a picture frame and set next to a special photograph of Brendan. My eyes fill with tears as I reflect upon these words of tenderness and love...Thank you, Danielle.**

The next poem I would like to share was beautifully and thoughtfully written by Brendan's cousin, Colleen Goddard Furey. It too, is a treasured keepsake, with her carefully chosen "words of love" beautifully written on her own special handcrafted white frame, with drawings of angels, pink and red roses, and two white doves, giving it a special touch of heaven. I have it propped up on a stand next to another favorite photo of Brendan. In September of

2003, we posted a copy of this poem on a tree at the cemetery, a few feet away from his memorial stone for all to see, where it still remains to this day. Colleen writes with love in her heart,

"I'll Remember"

I'll remember when you moved back from Arizona,

I'll remember your drums, Survivor, & The Eye of the Tiger.

I'll remember running through your house while it was being built, & exploring the woods behind when it was done.

I'll remember sleepovers at Eric's & staying up late. Laughing & goofing sometimes till daybreak.

I'll remember your smile and its slightly crooked shape. Your amazing compassion, always giving more than you'd take.

I'll remember your sense of humor, though not everyone got it.

I'll remember the Halloweens, the summers & the holidays. Forever in my heart, these moments will stay. Why you left I'll never understand, Though I know you're safe now, in God's hands.

I'll remember you forever & thank you each day, For the memories you've left that will be with me always. Your body is gone but your life will live on, in our hearts. The stories we'll tell, though sad at first, Will grow into the legacy you left while on earth. So though you are gone, I'll remember ….And always in my heart, you will live on.

I love you Brendan,
Love Always,
Colleen

Thank you Colleen, so much for your endearing,

descriptive message of love to Brendan. How wonderful it is to put these words into print! I am so grateful to you for this perfect opportunity to tell the world about him, my beloved son, who lives in our hearts with so many treasured memories. Yes…he's right here!!

(Colleen and Brendan were just one month apart in age).

This next poem was written by my younger sister, Angela. She and Brendan were always very close and her heart was sad and broken when his life was cut short. The following day, on September 12, 2003, she sat down in her quiet space, and with tears in her eyes, wrote the following poem while thinking of him.

"God's Newest Angel"

Take this time to lovingly see,
Our Angel, who's twenty seven;
His name is Brendan Michael McGee,
Who's now at peace in Heaven.
He made it home to God last night,
But couldn't say good bye;
He found his way through warmth and light,
And asks you not to cry.
Always keep your memories clear,
And always try to smile,
Because Brendan's standing very near,
And walks with us each mile.
He's happy now with Bob and Grace,
And waiting for the day,
When he will meet us face to face,
To guide us all the way.

Auntie Angela, 9/12/03

Thank you, Angela; You are a gift to me and will remain a gift to Brendan, as you continue to think of him and pray with him, blessed with the love you both shared. The Lord had another plan for him, much bigger than we can ever imagine, but we will continue to reminisce and confidently believe that he is here with us until our journey's end!

"Very interestingly," words I have spoken so often it seems, my sister, Angela, told me about a dream she had, on the exact night of my son Brendan's fatal accident.

"We were flying in the sky," she said to me, "and when we landed, we were birds! Brendan was a bluebird and I was a robin! While we were flying, we were people just like you and me, but when we landed, we said....Hey, we're birds!! And we couldn't stop laughing!"

This is a very strange dream, yet it is profoundly inspiring to me and the timing of it is also very interesting! There is so much we do not know regarding what actually happens when our spirit leaves our earthly body, but one day, I firmly believe, we will all be sitting together in a gigantic circle of love and will then understand, through the fulfillment of God's grace and glory!

I know this to be true when I read in 2 Corinthians 5:1 these words:

"For we know that when this tent we live in now is taken down---when we die and leave these bodies---we will have wonderful new bodies in heaven, homes that will be ours forevermore, made for us by God Himself and not by human hands."

Another very special person in Brendan's life was his godson, Stephen. Never did a birthday or holiday ever go by that Stephen's Uncle Brendan didn't surprise him with something very special for the occasion. It didn't matter what he brought; Stephen always loved and appreciated whatever it was his godfather had picked out for him. Being very grateful, he would always greet him with a big hug!! Actually, it was probably the highlight of Brendan's day as well, since he thoroughly enjoyed spending time with his godson.

In May of 2005, missing his godfather more than words could ever express, Stephen sat down and wrote a poem as he thought about his Uncle Brendan. Written on a special card he had made himself, complete with "rows of hearts" on all four sides of the card, he wrote these touching words of love:

"Caring"

Caring is Blue......
Like the sky.
It sounds like music,
It smells like roses,
It tastes like chocolate,
It looks like your smile.
Caring feels like love.
To Uncle Brendan,

Love, Stephen   5-14-05

(See photo)

Then he placed it on his godfather's memorial stone at the cemetery. I took a photo of this priceless card he had made so we would have it as a keepsake for many years to come, and could reflect upon and remember....Stephen's Uncle Brendan...."his idol," as he often called him. Stephen was just nine years old when he wrote this heartwarming poem to Brendan.

Thank you, Stephen, for sharing your deep and abiding love and admiration you have for your godfather, Brendan. I believe he will continue to watch over you every day of your life, because he loves you right back! Love is eternal; Love never dies.

Of special significance to me are the beautiful, yet powerful words to "An Irish Blessing." It was the song I chose for "the farewell hymn" at Brendan's funeral Mass on September 16, 2003. Today, seven years later, I remember so clearly, trying to express my love for him through the lyrics of this song, while tears streamed down my face. With God's love and strength, my husband and I walked along beside him, my arm draped across his casket as we made our way down the aisle.

As a tribute to him, I would like to conclude this page of my book with these words, precious to my heart........

AN IRISH BLESSING

"May the road rise to meet you.
May the wind be always at your back.
May the sun shine warm upon your face,
The rains fall soft upon your fields,
And, until we meet again,
May God hold you in the hollow of his hands."
I Love You so very much, Brendan.

LOVE ALWAYS, MOM.

Today, September 11, 2010, marks the seventh anniversary of my son's passing and the five o'clock Mass at St. Rose of Lima Church was offered in his remembrance.

After Mass, my twelve year old nephew, Thomas Wedge, presented me with a photograph I had given him seven years ago. It was the two of us, lighting a forever votive candle at the cemetery. Written above the photograph were his heartfelt words:

"Love is stronger than death even though it can't stop death from happening, but no matter how hard death tries, it can't separate people from love. It can't take away our memories either; in the end, life is stronger than death. Brendan will always be in that special place in our hearts, and will never be forgotten."

Thank you, Thomas, for being such a sweet and thoughtful person, always thinking of ways to help other people. I will cherish this "gift of love" always! (See photo)
Love,
Aunt Maggie.

Chapter 35 - Talking to God

After the unexpected loss of my son, Brendan, I realized I had no control over my life or the lives of those I love. Although I pray for them every day, their lives are ultimately in God's hands. I sincerely hope this prayer will minister to all who read this book and for those who still may be searching for answers after the loss of their son or daughter.

My Prayer of Surrender

Lord, I surrender all my cares, concerns and disappointments to you. I close my eyes and see you sitting beside me, waiting for me to hand over to you all that is heavy and burdensome upon my mind and heart. I really do want to surrender everything to you. Help me to accept my powerlessness and my need to control everything. Please remind me frequently that you are in control, because I often want to take *my* will back. I believe you have a plan and a purpose for everything that happens, although I often do not understand. Help me to surrender all control to you and to firmly believe you are the one in charge and that all things will work together for good. Your infinite love is immense and unfathomable. Why do I hesitate even though I envision your outstretched arms wanting to hold me? I hear you say, "I love you! Let go, let me release you of all that holds you in bondage. I am your freedom. I am your peace." Thank you, Jesus, my Wounded Healer for beckoning me to sit in silence with you as I listen attentively for your still small voice. Amen.

When Brendan left this world in September of 2003, a piece of my heart also went with him, but the Lord has continually provided me with the necessary graces I have needed to endure all my trials. Sometimes I reflect upon Scripture verses which speak personally to my heart. For example,
"Come to me all who are weary and I will give you rest" (Matthew 11:28) are words which often flash across my mind.

Another Scripture passage is, "The Lord is kind and merciful to all who call on Him" (Psalm 145:18).

Sometime after Brendan's passing, a close friend gave me the following prayer to read and reflect upon, and it has brought immeasurable healing for me a day at a time. I pray the words will also bring you the warmth of God's love. This prayer is written as follows:

"We seem to give our loved ones back to you Lord. You gave them to us. But just as you did not lose them in giving, neither do we lose them in return.

You don't give in the same way that the world gives. What you give you don't take away. You have taught us that what is yours is ours, also. Life is eternal, Lord and your love is undying. Death is only a horizon and a horizon is nothing but the limits of our sight.

Lift us, strong Son of God, that we may see farther. Cleanse our eyes that we may see more clearly. Draw us closer to yourself, that we may find ourselves closer to our loved ones who are with you.

And while you prepare a place for them, prepare us also for that happy place where you are and where we hope to be…forever. Amen."

(Author Unknown).

In February of 2005, I encountered Christ in a deeper and more intimate way through living cursillo. During this four day spiritual retreat, I received numerous letters of encouragement from people I had never met, who were praying for me throughout the weekend. Rosaries and other prayers were being offered for me. Sometime during that incredible weekend, I realized that Jesus had a plan for me and I knew He would be at my side through all of it. I feel God's love and mercy as I meditate upon this very meaningful prayer I received during my cursillo and I feel very inspired to pass it on to all of you. If you wish, invite the Lord, Jesus, into your heart as you pray these comforting words:

Heavenly Father, I call on you right now in a special way. It is through your power that I was created. Every breath I take, every morning I wake, and every moment of every hour, I live under your power.

Father, I ask you now to touch me with that same power. For if you created me from nothing, You can certainly recreate me. Fill me with the healing power of your Spirit. Cast out anything that should not be in me. Mend what is broken. Root out any unproductive cells. Open any blocked arteries or veins and rebuild any damaged areas. Remove all inflammation and cleanse any infection.

Let the warmth of your healing love pass through my body to make new any unhealthy areas so that my body will function the way You created it to function.

And Father, restore me to full health in mind and body so that I may serve You the rest of my life. I ask this through Christ our Lord. Amen.

In October of 2007, as I continued my journey of faith, I attended a very special retreat led by Father Andre Patenaude. The theme of the weekend was focused on the Eucharist and we were invited to reflect upon the words, "What does the Eucharist mean to you?"

After the death of my son, Brendan, I discovered that spending time in an adoration chapel, sitting before the Blessed Sacrament, brought me a deep inner peace. It was exactly where I needed and wanted to be. Nothing else could satisfy my longing to be with Brendan as I brought my pain and sadness before Jesus in the Blessed Sacrament. It was here I felt Brendan's presence and I could talk to him with the help of the Blessed Virgin Mary and her Son, Jesus. I knew they fully understood my pain and it brought me incredible comfort and a calming serenity and peace I can't even begin to describe.

I awoke very early in the morning and I read through the Gospel of Saint Luke, while pondering the words. When I wrote my explanation of what the Eucharist means to me, the answer was clearly written deep within my heart, soul and mind.

"What does the Eucharist mean to me?"

"It is the Gift of Eternal Life, Jesus, the Mighty, Holy One. It is the satisfaction of hungry hearts…my hungry heart. It is the guiding force to the Path of Peace. It is the Gift of Our Savior. It is the Kiss of Christ.

Each time I receive Jesus, it is a beautiful, intimate personal union and closeness; an adherence of my heart to Jesus' heart. It is indeed a foretaste of the Kingdom of God.

'Come,' my heart says, 'seek his face,' and I feel a longing to seek his face! Taste and see the goodness of the Lord. You have the words of Everlasting Life. For me, the Eucharist is a Healing Remedy for my mind, body and spirit."

Since that weekend, I have been drawn to a deeper union with my loving Savior whom I can depend upon for everything.

A year and four months later, in February of 2009, my husband and I attended a weekend retreat which we began to attend each year following our cursillo weekend in 2005. Throughout the weekend we read and reflected upon the 150 psalms as written in the Bible and were invited to write our own personal "Psalm 151" which I wrote as follows:

"Psalm 151"

"In the early morning hours Lord, my soul searches for you and I hear your loving voice calling back to me.

As I surrender my brokenness and hurts to you, I know you hear all my prayers.

Being one with you and being united to you is my healing grace and I am cleansed of the poison of resentment, anger, guilt and fear. You are my comfort as you walk by my side.

I put on my helmet of salvation and ask you to direct my thinking away from self-pity, self-will, dishonest and self-seeking motives. I put on my breastplate of righteousness and my garment of praise as I ask you to guard my emotions. I put on my belt of truth and know You are the Way, the Truth and the Life. I put on my boots of peace and walk as a well-armed soldier. I take with me, my shield of faith and the sword of the Spirit, which is the word of God.

Only goodness and mercy will follow me all the days of my life and I will one day enter heaven, my real home to be with You and my loved ones forever. I praise and I thank You Jesus, for your awe-inspiring love, patience and kindness. Amen."

Finally, I would like to close this chapter of my book with a verse from the Bible, which has popped up repeatedly, time and time again, no matter what book I open to read. I believe the Lord is speaking to me directly, while walking by my side and helping me to stay on track.

Rejoice always; pray without ceasing; in everything give thanks; for this is God's will for you in Christ Jesus
(1 Thessalonians 5:16-18).

ABOUT THE AUTHOR

I am the third born in a family of thirteen children. My parents carefully chose our names, each one with special significance. During my high school years, I became known as "Maggie," by my circle of friends, co-workers, and family members. However, today I truly appreciate the name given by my parents on the day of my birth. That name is Margaret Catherine. Thanks Mom and Dad!

I began caring for my younger siblings at about the age of nine. From the time I can remember, it was my job to gather the family for morning prayers. Arousing my brothers in the morning was never an easy task! "The family that prays together, stays together," are words I remember reading as a young girl, as our family knelt down to pray. We have always been a close knit family and the loss of Brendan was devastating to all of us.

I always enjoyed going to Mass and other church services with my parents. Some of my fondest memories are those special moments attending benediction services at a small chapel with my dad. Even as a young girl, I remember how I always felt a calming peacefulness whenever I was there. Already, the Lord was speaking to my heart and perhaps this was the beginning of my journey of faith.

My decision to become a nurse was made when I was just five years old. I knew it then, and it was all I ever wanted to be! My decision was solid! My career as a registered nurse was very rewarding and fulfilling. Forty-three years later, I made a conscious and well thought out decision to retire.

After my son died in 2003, I knew the Lord was directing me down a different path. Seven years had passed, and in January of 2010, I knew His plan and new purpose for me was to look through my journals and enter my many powerful and profound experiences into a book, to be shared with others. It was a way of helping others in a new and different way; not just within the confines of the hospital where I had worked. Now was the appointed time to write my thoughts on paper for all to read and be ministered to in a special and profound way. Using what was so freely given to me, including my strong faith and one spiritual experience after another, I had a passion to share with others, which brings me to the present day. Then a surge of energy burst forth in my heart to make it a reality and the writing began.

Indeed, I will attribute the success of my book to the honor and glory of God, who instilled within my heart a dream and a passion to write this book and to reach out to other parents who are searching for answers to their many questions, such as, "Will I really see my son again? Will I recognize him or her? Will we know each other? What will he look like? Is heaven real? Why did God let this happen? How will I cope when sometimes I can't even breathe? Will my heart ever feel at peace again?"

I feel driven in a very powerful way to speak to the many sorrowing hearts because I have been there. I can feel their heartache and hopefully, I can answer their questions and offer support, thereby alleviating the yearnings of their hearts so they will find peace.

Like words flashing through my mind, I often hear the Lord saying to me, "It is not you who chose me, but it is I who chose you."

With gratitude in my heart, I would like to thank you for reading my book. Perhaps you have identified with one or more of my stories, through your own personal experiences.

If you are interested in sending me your comments, it would be a joy to hear from you. My email address is heisrightherebymaggie@gmail.com.

May God's peace be with you always,

Maggie (Margaret) McGee.